260 Queens Quay West
Suite 1102
Toronto, Ontario
Canada M5J 2N3

Cover design: Lara Vanderheide
Interior design: Lara Vanderheide
Editing: Anna Watson

Distribution:
NewLeaf Distribution
401 Thorton Rd.
Lithia Springs, GA 30122-1557
ISBN: 978-1-927005-41-5

Printed and bound in The United States of America

Dedications

To my dear parents

Dolores & Gualberto Abelgas

&

My first born son

Traehnel

Acknowledgements

First and foremost I'd like to God for getting me through such a tremendous journey, for without Him I would not be able to achieve this dream. To Sanjay Burman, CEO of Burman Books / my publisher thank you so much for opening the doors and believing in me. To my wonderful editor Anna Watson, I'm so grateful for your guidance, thank you. To my close family and friends who supported and believed in me from day one; you've all given me the strength to follow through. To my beautiful niece Reya Anne, you are my ray of sunshine, I'm so proud to be your Auntie. And last but not least, my three beautiful sons, my angels on earth Traehnel, Yahsua & Zach; my #1 supporters – you guys are my rock, mommy loves you so much.

xo

Honey Lou

July 2014

To

Mary Grace & Sharleen,

Stay beautiful and go
after what you want...

Regards
Honeylon

Table of Contents

INTRODUCTION

Hello, my name is Honey Lou

"True religion is real living; living with all one's soul, with all one's goodness and righteousness."

Albert Einstein

What is it in all of us – what do you say about the soul? How did it even come about? What is the soul? Does it even exist? Where did it come from and if the soul does exist, then why are we here? Why aren't we living the soul? I've had the very same questions in the back of my head. I can't tell you based on what I've researched – I'm not an expert – but I can tell you I *am* the research and I know that the soul is more alive than we think.

I've been aware of my journey as a soul being since I was around six months old. I was consciously aware that I was a being in a body.

Since then, it's been my journey to discover life and find its meaning.

At that age I discovered I was very much alive, crying, kicking and screaming but there was something else trapped inside of me. I was in a body that I couldn't control. I was a trapped soul and there was nothing I could do. The oldest memory I have as a six month old baby, I remember crying, like a little baby who was hungry, tired, and uncomfortable or in a need of a diaper change. I stared right in the eyes of a dark-haired woman; I knew who she was but at the same time I didn't. She looked as if she was doing everything she could to help me. All I felt was pain; I needed a diaper change because my little bottoms were hurting me. I was angrily screaming at her.

Then all of a sudden, it was like a shift so fast that until this day I still can't understand what triggered it. I started screaming and yelling but there was someone else inside me. One was crying and the other was frustrated, trying to get their voice across. "Hello don't you understand, I am in pain, help me, my bum hurts!" I screamed in despair. "What don't you guys understand? Do you understand English – and hello can you hear me?" But the words were coming out as a loud cry, the more I yelled, the angrier my cry sounded. What was this? Why couldn't I communicate like I used to? Where was I?

I then realized that I was trapped. The words coming out of my mouth weren't coming across; rather they came out as a ferocious cry. It was as if I was so far away but yet, I was right there. I remember that moment. That was the moment I realized I was a helpless little baby. I recall saying to myself, "Wow, I'm back here."

Staring through my own eyes as if it was gazing through a window, I felt I was some kind of vessel and that my driver had just abandoned me. I stared and stared, and then it was done. I was very much alive but in a new body; I then realized I was born again. I don't remember any other episodes like that ever since but I do remember it clear as day and it it's always been in the back of my head. I have carried that memory and it keeps my spirit moving towards unlocking more truths.

Ever since that episode, I've known that I was different. I felt different and I can tell that people could see that I was also different; sometimes it would make me feel uncomfortable but never insecure. As I was growing up I always felt like an odd ball around other kids, as if I was the weird one.

I've always felt some sort of entitlement, not the kind of entitlement that spoiled kids are born into. For lack of better words, it was a divine entitlement – knowing that I'm human, that I'm not perfect and that life is a learning experience. I'm only here temporarily so I have to fulfill my mission.

I don't think like others do and I'm able to pick up on people's energy and know their purpose, destiny, joy and pain etc. It's almost as if I could easily connect with their soul and spirit. Like I knew something they didn't.

I've lived with what I used to think was a curse and a gift. Sometimes, I just don't want to know and would prefer to live with a blind eye. I was as conscious and aware as Silvia Browne, the famous psychic who just recently passed, trying to live life like a normal person, but no matter what I did, I couldn't ignore what I already knew. My spiritual growth was very important to me. Often I come across people who are in search of this path later in their life. I've been fortunate enough to have empowered my spiritual self and now I have embraced it as a gift.

There are so many things that have happened in my life that it's hard to ignore and argue with. It just makes you want to dig deeper than the 24 hours that we breathe.

For instance, when my eldest son was about two and a half years old, I was up writing on the computer. I had plumped him in front of the television to watch his favourite late night TV show, hoping he would fall asleep. About 45 minutes had passed, I was so deep into my writing that I almost forgot we were in the same room. I turned to look at him to check if he had fallen asleep. Before I could even softly finish calling his name, you wouldn't believe what I saw; I stopped breathing for a brief second. He was asleep on his stomach and his head was facing the same direction as me. There on top of his head was a big bright halo, a perfect circle and as bright as a light bulb. I couldn't believe what I was seeing but I wasn't frightened at all. I felt warm inside and something in me just knew to accept it as it is. I heard a little voice that said "Nurture him, he's an Angel." Then this feeling of knowing came over me; I can't even describe what it was like. It felt like an inner validation of my purpose. Certain things just made sense as if another piece of the puzzle had been found. Even after turning back and forth to make sure I wasn't seeing things, the halo sat perfectly still above his head for about three minutes. On a physical, emotional and spiritual level, there's always been something that follows me to remind me of where I came from and that I'm nothing but a soul spirit having a human experience.

My teachers used to tell me that I was a very unique person, but every time they'd say that I didn't know whether to feel like a bigger weirdo or feel special. I remember when I used to get sick; I hated it. I didn't understand what was happening. It was scary, but at the same time I thought it was pretty cool. I would see myself lying there as if I was someone else.

I'd travel to different places, where the stars were just shooting past me as fast as light. I dodged different sized objects that looked like meteoroids. Then, as I gradually got better, I would come back to my body.

Sounds pretty far-fetched, but that's what I went through as a child every time I was sick. The moment I closed my eyes, I'd leave my body and have lucid dreams. Could you imagine? All my life I thought this was normal. I had the ability to control my dreams.

In one dream, I opened a door and someone tried to shoot me. In the middle of my dream, I stopped it and said, "Oh no, this is my dream and there's no way it's going to go down like this." So I would re-start at the point back to when I opened the door, but this time, I was able to change it so whoever was trying to get me wouldn't get the opportunity to.

My dreams are always very insightful and often manifest in life, which again keeps me searching for answers. Almost every single dream I've had either comes true, or a spirit talks to me to give me messages full of meaning and visions of which probably 98% have come true.

My aunt Rita came through in one dream I had recently. She had come to give me a message. She said that someone was trying to go against the will of the dead (she was talking about her will that she left with my mom). She made it clear to tell my mother and her sister that someone was trying to take their property; the property my mother inherited from her. She said, "This land has been cursed by the blood, sweat and tears of her and all the ancestors." She continued, "Whoever tries to go against this will, will have consequences and they will not succeed."

A few days later, I went to visit my mom. I couldn't wait to tell her my dream because I knew that this was a message. I began to relay the message to my mother, before I could even finish, she ran to the phone and called her other sister to tell her what I just said. Even though my mother's accepted my gifts, she still gets flabbergasted. Overhearing her conversation with my aunt, I was validated. See, my mom is very secretive and I'm not sure why. She had just received news from her sister about a month or so ago that their cousin was trying to take the property and had begun the process.

I had no idea this was happening at all, or even had the hunch. So, there you go. My dreams are my dreams and they are full of messages.

Life as a wife and mother of three keeps me distracted from trying to decode all my dreams and the overwhelming feeling of guilt.

"I could have done this."

"I should have done that."

In all honesty, I think if I was single and didn't have any children, this would be my life, decoding my dreams and travelling different parts of the world; just questioning. There's always been something inside me that gives me that happy feeling when it comes to the mysteries of our planet, world/dimension; it fascinates me.

That feeling of freedom and eternal love resides deep down in me. I still long to get out of my body at night when the world feels too heavy. There's nothing like feeling eternal, timeless, endless space and contentment. No hate, no jealousy, no envy, no anger, no evil, no negative thoughts, and it feels as if you're one with everything. Knowing this kind of feeling has humbled me quite a bit. It's taught me compassion, to be more compassionate for people who I don't know.

Could you imagine feeling one with all? Imagine a world of people living life awakened, knowing their gifts and the universal love of being one with all. Where we would have a constant mutual understanding for one another; where love and forgiveness is automatic... No titles, no rich, no poor, no hunger, no beauty, no ugliness, just people awakened in truth and love.

That is the fire that burns inside me, the fire that keeps me strong when times are tough in this world. It keeps me going because I know there is something greater than you and I and I have to keep the fire burning if I want to get there. There's always been this sense of love that dwells in me. I often wonder if I'm just a soul who came back to spread love; I am part of this loving universal vibration, like I'm here to help maintain the energy.

The fire that burns inside me is all from my heart; I can be very passionate, which is a big part of my life because it has helped me to heal each time. I am on a mission in life to fulfill my destiny and I believe my soul has a greater purpose. My blueprint has already been written and I'm here to complete it. We all have a blueprint that must be completed. It's what we came here for and I believe we all have a purpose in this life. God will reveal it to us when we're ready to depart and cross over.

I want to share my story and inspire young women across the globe through the lessons life has taught me. While everyone was in school getting an education, life was teaching me some valuable lessons. I am here to complete a mission, whatever that mission is; I just want to be heard. It's like that young spirit in me as a baby, trying to get my point across. I feel like that was the first piece of the puzzle. Most people like me who have that activist mentality, we just want someone to hear us and understand us and that's our biggest challenge. We want to make a difference, but how?

I know that there is something greater than ourselves which guides and protects us if we will just listen and pay attention.

I hope that by the end of this book, you too can be awakened to loving your soul, to find the meaning of who you are, your purpose and your destiny and to become a positive influence to this world; to join the vibration of love.

I believe that I am a light worker sent here to set people free, to awaken them to their true selves. We all share the same 24 hours, we all breathe the same air and one thing's for sure, at the end of this life journey – I know that we answer to only one God.

CHAPTER 1

The Blueprint

*"Cherish your visions and your dreams
as they are the children of your soul, the
blueprints of your ultimate achievements."*

Napoleon Hill

Have you heard of the word "blueprint"? We make blueprints
for projects that we want to complete. To me a BLUEPRINT is a
road map of our life – our life is the project. I'm pretty sure the
word itself has fluttered by our ears a few times before but we
don't really know the depth of it. When we came into this earth
plane we had already written the chapters of our life on a scroll
which we can now call The Blueprint.

Our soul, each human being on earth, you and I are the authors
of this book called Life. I am a firm believer in God and He is our
co-author and editor; then we're given a chance to publish it on
earth.

I remember, once through my spiritual awakening, my spirit
guide told me exactly how it worked. Imagine, I literally woke
up the next day, knowing about the universal laws; odd part
was, it's like I was already aware of this knowledge and I was

now just remembering it. It's like I had dementia for years and I was starting to remember – but I'll talk more about my spiritual awakening in the following chapters.

Life is a flowing river that sparkles from the sun and we jump into it, our souls that is. Birth is when the soul comes alive. We come here on this earth plane with a mission, our Blueprint is our map. When coincidences happen, they're not really a coincidence but something that was meant to be.

There's a few glitches in the time capsule and sometimes we see patterns, like for some odd reason you always seem to look at the clock when it's at either 11:11, 2:22 , 4:44 and so on. These are little patterns in life that give us a reminder of what we're meant to do. Ever since I became aware of such coincidences and patterns, it was like a tap on the shoulder of either, wake up look around you or keep on going you're on the right track. It's never really good to go against the grain either, I always say, you can't force the force or there's consequences you have to pay.

Here's a short story.

I was about 17 years old. I had my awakening when I was 16 years old, and from that moment, my spirit guide had told me I was going to be writing a book. So, I started doing some automatic writing. I knew this was automatic writing because after reading what I had written, there was no way I could've known what had been written without being one with the Universe. Many PhD's and great writers have written identical things years before I was even born – like I said, it was like having dementia and remembering again.

It was about 10:30pm and I had received a phone call from a (not so good) friend to go hang out and party. The minute I hung up the phone, I closed my eyes and tried to get some spiritual insights from my spirit guide, whether I should go or not. She told me not to go out that night and that I should stay home or else there would be consequences.

Typical teenager, I was like, yeah okay, I don't even listen to my mother, and I'm now supposed to listen to my spiritual mom. I mean I believed it all, but I was being a stubborn Gemini and I went against the grain. So, I left in middle of writing, saved my work and continued to get dressed. The work I saved was about three months' worth of writing, keep that in mind. I go out and I actually had a really bad night (go figure). My mind wasn't there at all. I came home at about 3:30am from the party. I didn't drink or anything because I had no money (those were the days when we only needed $5 for gas money and to try to get in the club before a certain time so it would be free). I didn't even undress; I went straight to the computer with some guilt that built up while I was out. To my surprise, EVERYTHING was deleted – the file was missing, not a single trace. Recycling bin, computer search, nothing came up and for weeks I was searching. I even accused my siblings of going on my computer, even though nobody knew my password. I was totally bummed. It was three hard months – what could've been a masterpiece – destroyed without a trace. Gone without an explanation, I was dazed.

That was a lesson learned – that you can't go against the grain. Sometimes, life already has it planned out for you. When it's part of your destiny and set in stone in your Blueprint and you keep trying to avoid it or run from it, it will follow you. What happens to a flower when it doesn't get enough water? Our wellbeing will start to crumble. We die inside. We become indecisive, get health problems and there's always that feeling of being incomplete – when the miracle you've been waiting for is right in front of you. You run away from it, it will continue to get you. After that incident, I learned to ground myself, listen to my spirit guide and my intuitions a bit more. Our spirit guides are there to help us through this journey and path we've mapped out. For that I am thankful and blessed.

Take a minute right now to just breathe in and breathe out.

We are more than just beings; we taste, see, hear and more importantly feel. Our Blueprint is triggered by certain scenarios in life, such as meeting a person, a place, sound or an object. Some call it déjà vu. Déjà vu is almost like a check point, little reminders that "oh yeah" – you have already been there before.

The minute we are born, we're at the most conscious peak and I believe we go back to that state on our last dying days. This is why we hear so many stories that seem far-fetched from people who already know they're ready to pass. Our senses at birth are at their highest frequency but unfortunately as years pass by on this earth our memory gets diluted by society and we forget the true meaning of our journey and existence. Elaborating on how society affects our consciousness would be another book in itself.

The earth is divided into different realms and dimensions where other higher spiritual beings dwell. White light entities such as angels, guides and protectors are also connected to us, operating in the higher vibration. We would look as if we're the ghosts in their dimension. We operate in the lower dimension, which means also at a lower frequency but we're evolving, growing and waking up – and in my Blueprint it's part of my job to help others aboard the jet plane.

We as spiritual beings wrote our Blueprint with a story and a purpose. Things in our lives just don't happen; we don't meet and cross paths for no reason. Everything is put there so we can learn and experience it. Life is when an entity is born to earth and given a will to live. At that very moment when we are given life, we have been blessed; just the simplicity of being able to experience the beauty of LIFE, it's definitely a gift from the Divine. Life is a magnificent creation by God. It is one of many that are miraculous, mysterious and beautiful. This is why we have to always remind ourselves that no matter how hard life is, we created this, so let's learn to trust in ourselves and gain control. There's way too many of us who aren't thankful for opportunities we get and we abuse them because we are ignorant. I believe that if you know the root and the deeper meaning of our existence and purpose, you'll have a clearer view, a much better understanding and the knowledge to master ourselves; the art of ONE. Remember after all, you wrote it – you have to trust in yourself.

The Awakening

I've been blessed to experience such bliss that I almost had no choice but keep questioning and searching for answers and the only way I was going to get the answers was by living them all. You can't keep running away, because eventually, whatever you're running from will keep repeating itself until you learn to face it.

I was only 14 years old when I became pregnant, but let me tell you by listening to my heart I did the right thing by keeping my child. That was when I learned to follow my intuition. If I don't feel it my heart, then I won't do it, and if I do go against the grain there's always a price to pay – that's what consequences mean. For every action, there's a consequence and consequences are either good or bad, depending on the energy you put into the universe.

After going through the worst time of life when I tried to end my own life (I can still recall that period, because now I am thankful for it,) I was going through an awakening. It was almost as if it was forced on me like a huge windstorm that I had to trek through. Things in my life started to be different. I found myself more sensitive around other people. I started to hear things.

We were going on a family vacation to my motherland, the entire family including my son. I think this is when it hit me. Somehow this vacation opened my perspective on life at only 16 years old. I remember seeing real poverty for the very first time. It was the worst feeling but it awakened my heart and soul. This is where I was born, where I spent the first six years of my life –

this could have been me.

So many thoughts and emotions were going through me this entire trip that I couldn't understand them. Why are there children on the streets as young as my son (two years old), living in a cardboard box, begging for change? Why is this woman on the street with all her kids? Is this life? All I remember feeling was my heart wanting to jump out and reach out – and that feeling alone was enough for me to want to figure things out. I was beginning to feel alive, and even more thankful for the life I was living, although I didn't have much. The more I was thankful and the more I showed gratitude towards life, the more receptive I was getting. I felt as if I was exchanging with the universe. I am thankful for you, and in return the universe slowly opened my third eye and blessed me with abundance.

One night, we stayed at my aunt's place, which was over 100 years old. It was time for bed. I remember not being able to sleep that night because I had felt a presence. Heck, I didn't know what "presence" meant or felt like. But I started to hear whispers and felt people around me and they were starting to manifest. I started to see them through a different eye as if they were there, I see them, but at the same time they weren't there too. The feelings were manifesting; I felt people, now people were slowly starting to show themselves – I was scared as shit. I jumped from the other side of the room onto my sister's bed and slept on her foot (mind you, this is half a single bed made of bamboo, so you can only imagine how comfortable it was). She asked me what my problem was and I replied, "They're staring at me." The next morning we never spoke about it; I was still confused. This is the house I grew up in. I remember flying over the roof and I remember seeing people at night, talking and laughing. When you were only a toddler, everything seemed real, but it was all starting to make sense to me – I've always had a gift.

Now, this didn't just disappear…. It got stronger. We had flown back home from our vacation. Everything else was a blur to me. I got home and I literally kissed my bed, the floor, my computer, everything in the house. My perspective changed. From feeling that the world hated me, vice versa, and I wasn't worthy of living and nobody loved me to being so thankful and happy. I came back so full of life and valuing it. I wanted to LIVE, as if I felt I had a purpose now – I was on a HIGH.

My entire perspective changed. As weeks went by, the gifts were getting stronger. The voice followed me around. It was a woman's voice, very soft and clear but distant. I thought I had an over active imagination but I knew I was far from crazy, so I paid attention to it. The more I paid attention to it, I started to notice the difference in my own thoughts and when she spoke. They were two different people. I know, it sounds crazy but we ALL have this – a spirit guide, call it a tour operator. She would teach me things. I was lying in bed one night and I really wanted to tap in; keep in mind, I had no idea what I was doing but something in me guided me.

I asked, "Who are you, and what is your name?"

She replied, "Sing-ha, I am your great grandmother."

Okay, I was fully having a conversation with someone I couldn't see. Was I scared? Oddly enough no. She started to show me her life and who she was to me, the role she played in my life and what she was here for. She told me she was here for me. I'm the chosen one. What did she mean the chosen one, I'm thinking? Was I going to be like Mother Theresa and become a saint because I wasn't ready for that? All jokes aside, I was really stunned. Chosen? Maybe chosen in the family, in this generation, I don't know. All she said was that I have no choice because this was my calling and she would guide me through it. What I was about to go through nobody will understand.

The next morning, I questioned my mother, a little Q&A pow-wow to validate my conversation with my newfound spirit guide/great-grandmother– Singha. Later I found out her real name was Soprana; close enough.

After telling my mother that her grandmother showed up to me and told me everything she had been through in her life (that I couldn't have possibly had any knowledge of – not even mom), my mom had a worried look on her face as if I had gone mad. For some reason I thought she'd be curious and intrigued but instead, she was worried for me.

I mean now I don't blame her. A lot had happened within the year – I tried to end my life, I ran away and now I'm talking to her deceased grandmother. I was going through my awakening and she was going through a shock.

I started distancing myself from others, friends and family. I found myself meditating more. Every day, she would teach me little things, how to feel the earth's vibration and then how to let go of it when I've absorbed too much. She taught me how to read rocks. I would be able to connect with her through intense meditation.

Here I am, an urbanite teen who should be out drinking and partying (I cut all that out during that time, right after I came home from our family vacation, also red meat, my spirit guide told me, meat was not good for the body, it blocks energy) . I wanted to know more. Everything in this universe started to make sense. I saw the beauty in everything and in everyone; the loving vibration of energy that we're all capable of giving. I was so high on life.

I started reading books and one of them was by James Redfield called *The Celestine Prophecy* and (my bible) *The Inner Treasure: An Introduction to the World's Sacred and Mystical Writings* by Jonathan Star. While reading the books, my body would literally vibrate – it was validation after validation. Through the books, I didn't feel alone anymore. This was universal knowledge that's been written about for thousands of years. Since I couldn't talk to anyone about my experiences, I turned to books.

As weeks passed, my mother started getting really concerned about me. She had taken me to the doctor to get me assessed and I went along with it. My spirit guide had mentioned to me days before that my mother would be taking me to the doctor and told me not to listen to what the doctor said. She said, "Do not take the pills; nobody will understand what you're going through." She was very firm and stern that I must listen to her – without giving it a thought, I did. I remember sitting down at the doctor's office and the doctor asked me some questions. Then she pulled her pen and pad and said, "She is going through depression; here I will prescribe her Prozac to take for a month." A quick fix, right on Doc! I could see from my mother's face that she felt some relief as she tried to force a fake smile. As soon as I got home, without hesitation I proceeded straight to the washroom and threw the pills in the garbage.

Back then I had no idea what the logic was behind that, but now as a consciously aware adult, I get it. We are so quick to turn to drugs to fix problems in our society. I'm not ignoring the fact that there are people who genuinely need medication to help them with an illness. If we're having relationship issues, the doctor tells you you're depressed and puts you on some kind of anti-depressant. You're basically not any different from someone who first started using hard drugs to numb the pain, but in this case it's a legal drug. You're incoherent to your problems, thinking it's gone away and as soon as reality kicks in, you're looking to numb the pain again with pills. What will happen when that anti-depressant is all gone, you're still faced with the same problem and it gets bigger the more you bury it? We're digging our own graves.

I'm just saying, be fierce and take it one day at a time. Like the Buddhist who believes that life by nature is already difficult, imperfect and complex, try looking for answers within ourselves first. If I had suppressed the force with anti-depressant pills, I'd probably be really messed up right now and it would follow me , confuse me and I'd   be an empty soul with heavy baggage – not healthy.

OBE

That evening, exhausted from my adventure, I went to my bed and lay there. Then something strange started happening to me when I closed my eyes. I don't know how long it was from the time I closed my eyes but I started hearing loud drums – like tribal drums. It was so loud that I said to myself, "Who in the world is banging drums so late at night; this can wake up the entire neighborhood?" The strange part was that I was asleep, but awake and I wasn't really in my bed. I was coming out of my bed. I yelled for my mom, "Momma, Momma!" Then all of a sudden, my body started vibrating, like little electro magnets were pinching my skin. I then started to feel as if something was pulling me from my bed towards the ceiling; as if I was elastic and getting sucked up by a massive suction. I was getting really scared. Then all of a sudden, boom, I shot up over the roof.

This wasn't a dream, this was real. I saw myself lying there. I remember thinking I was dead. "This is what death feels like," I thought. I'm not sure how long it lasted but I didn't want to go any further. Then I was back into my body. I stared at the ceiling, I touched my chest, my arms and took a deep breath – I was alive, phew! As scary as it sounds, that was one of the best spiritual adventures that's ever happened to me. I was more convinced that there's so much more in life than our physical body. We are a soul with a spirit, having a human experience. I woke up the next day, and I wrote about it.

This is a poem I wrote after my first Out of the Body experience – written over 10 years ago.

I lay awake in a meditated state, third eye awakened to heaven's gate

Souls of the lost and found, watched my fragile body from above the ground

I asked my spiritual guidance to take over my body as I roam the planes in silence

Cold air lifted my conscience, as she supersede

No thoughts for my mind to feed

My spirit wanting to explore OBE, as I'm taken over sub-consciously

Native entities, descend with me, like their souls are living through me
I saw myself rising above the fire, Indian summer
My conscious twitching, took me to see a dimension, in different forms of expansion
Fear of not waking, lights flashed before me, like God is waiting
Floating like a ghost in lost space, haunting where it never took place

*My spirit guide laid in me as I was trying to get back, it
came so quick like the first beam of light, to morning from
night, early bright sight
I tried to catch it, to make it home, back to my mental
dome, where they love and give*

*I woke up feeling not to fear but wanting to understand,
what was never taught by man
Apalachee taught me, that my will is to survive, the wolf
cries, the earth energies, you give lies, it will despise,
what's not to emphasize, Apalachee taught me to realize,
look far beyond dark skies*

After that evening, I almost felt like I was blessed with
something – the knowledge of the universe. I was given a
plethora of knowledge – simple little things like if you're going to
be mean to others it'll come back to you in different ways. You
lie; you're going to be lied to much worse. But the generous part
of it is, when you love, you will receive love back 100 times over.
I started doing my research on Out of Body experiences – I was
relieved to find there were so many more. I'm not the only crazy
one after all.

So many things have happened to me on a spiritual level. Some
say I am a seer, a light worker, a psychic but to me, I feel like
everyone has it in them, so I'm no different. Maybe it's because
I wanted to know this mystery; I didn't run away from it. This
was about a decade ago and it's still happening today. The world
is changing, and a lot of people will be experiencing this bliss. I

say, we embrace it. It all leads to love and understanding – it's what the world needs. The vibration is shifting and at times, it feels as if it's a battle between good and bad – but like all things, LOVE is the answer.

By knowing the meaning of existence and by accepting that we are more than just a body but a mere soul having a human experience, you will see that our lives may, just maybe start to make a lot of sense and the things and people we love around us too. Then, we can be more perceptive to so many things, and most importantly, the valuable lessons that life teaches us. As much as at times, the load feels more of a burden that hinders us from our dreams more than anything else; you have to learn to trust in GOD that he does not put forth what you cannot handle.

Here is a small exercise I do in gratitude to the universe.

Try closing your eyes, take a deep breath and while you inhale, exhale with a smile. Envision what a perfect world would be like, when everyone is full of love– does it look like heaven?

Then say this Ho'ponono prayer that my Reiki Tummo master introduced me to: *Please forgive me, I am sorry, I love you, thank you.*

Keep that thought and remember that only through love and prayer we as human beings can bring peace into this world – stop war, save a life and stop natural disasters from happening. Pray and meditate daily.

Love and light.

CHAPTER 2

Heart Backwards

"I lived in that solitude which is painful in youth, but delicious in the years of maturity."

Albert Einstein

Here's a story of how I met my first son's dad; it was an important chapter of my life because it taught me love in its different variations. Not only that but I learned to understand that there's no greater love than God's love and whatever will be, will be.

We'd known each other since I was 11 years old. We watched each other grow into the person we are today – and truthfully speaking for myself, he did have some influence in the person I have become. Do you believe in soul mates, twin flames and past lives? Well whether you do believe it or not, I feel in my heart that we've shared a life prior to this one and we vowed to come back this lifetime – but that doesn't mean there's always going to be a happy ending. We can come back for karmic reasons.

I remember the first time we met through friends. My girlfriends and I had gone down to their school to hang out. He had heard about me through his friends. They told him that they had met this girl at track & field named Honey Lou (first name Honey, middle name Lou). The boys from his school had a crush on me and they'd talk about me to him but so typical of him, he didn't jump on the bandwagon right away and he wanted to see me for himself.

I remember that day like it was yesterday. It was the perfect summer day, the sun was out and the sky was clear. My girlfriends and I had taken the bus to go to hang out with the other kids from his school. When got off the bus we were met by a boy named Terry who liked me and I kind've liked him back. He said we were going to meet up with his buddy aka my future son's dad. As we were walking we caught up with a couple of guys walking up the street. I will never forget that day, because I knew that this guy we were going to meet was going to be a part of me forever. There's a feeling that sticks with you. It's a feeling that almost makes you complete, like finding the missing puzzle piece. It just felt right, like we were two in the same; a sense of wholeness.

"Hey, this is Honey," his friend introduced us. The world stopped for a split-second. I looked his two-toned eyes and I knew right away that this guy was my twin flame; it felt like I was reconnected to a familiar soul behind those eyes. The world paused as nobody else was around us and instantaneously we felt this strong connection. I think I fell in love and so did he. We were 11 and 12 year old kids; what did we know, except for that feeling we felt for each other?

Well, we became only good friends after that. I even tried hooking him up with my girlfriends. During this entire time, we wanted to be with each other but we were just friends and nothing more. We spent most of our days together as friends, late nights on the phone nonstop – hiding our true feelings from each other. The chemistry was growing between us and our friendship was getting deeper. I can still remember when I used to look forward to the evening time because I knew that was the time he'd call me. Well, not quite, we had a mutual friend, who we'd get to call first just so it didn't make it obvious that we really wanted to talk to each other. So, we'd play it off and asked our mutual friend to "three-way" us in the call. Then, we'd somehow end up getting rid of the mutual friend and it would just be him and me all night, regardless if we had school the next day. I was already head over heels for him; I was madly deeply in love. Who's to say you can't fall in love at a young age? It was pure. It wasn't something that wasn't forced, it was innocent and it just happened without realizing it.

After a year of playing the "we're only friends" game and being that extra-close, close friend we ended up telling each other exactly how we felt on December 28, 1997. That was only the beginning of what was yet to come; nothing would ever be the same. We were in love, deeply in love and dangerously out of control. We needed to see each other, hear each other's voice every day – the relationship got so serious and we didn't even know it. I personally believe that everyone has that important piece of memory of their first love, whether we're with them or not. There's just something that will never feel the same ever; a space reserved in your heart for that special person who first touched it.

My situation took a slight turn and ended up different from the rest of your typical girl meets boy story. Two weeks after my 14th birthday, I became pregnant. That's right, I was only 14 and we started having sex three months into our relationship. I'd barely graduated from elementary school, not even close to starting high school yet. It was the summer of 1998 when I missed two months of my menstrual period. The biggest regret I ever had in my life was breaking up with him – while pregnant and I didn't even have a clue. I had started to feel like I was way too young to be committed to someone for the rest of my life. The way things were going, I didn't want to be in a serious relationship anymore – I broke up with him not knowing I was already 8 weeks pregnant.

I was in the state of crisis. That was the first time I've ever felt the pain of regret. I was selfish then and I didn't realize what I was doing. There was my first love, and I broke his heart because I didn't want to be committed anymore. Even though it didn't feel right, I went against my heart. I was a child, I obviously didn't know any better. Had I known I was already pregnant, I would've never done what I did.

Back in the day we didn't have Google so instead we used the Yellow Pages. I found a Catholic-based place for women who either think they're pregnant or are pregnant. I subconsciously chose this place because I knew they were Catholic and they were going to encourage me to keep the baby and possibly talk me out of having an abortion. Aborting my child was out of the question and never crossed my mind – but first the test result had to come back positive.

Deep down inside, I wanted someone to say, "Don't abort it" and to not judge me; I was definitely looking for approval. I didn't waste any time and made the appointment the following day. I remember being greeted by a soft spoken woman; her hair was very well kept as if she took her time every morning to do it. She told my friend and me to have a seat while they examined my urine test. While we were in this Victorian-style room, an abortion video played on a TV in the background. I don't really remember what I was thinking but was trying to block all thoughts and emotions from entering my mind. After briefly seeing the video, there was no way in hell I was in the mental or emotional state to make that life changing decision – hell I haven't lived enough to really know what goes on in life. I was brought up as a Catholic and all my life I was taught that it was bad and that I'd go to hell if I ever had an abortion.

Shortly after she came back into the room, based on her body language and the look on her face, I got this weird feeling right in the pit of my stomach to my chest and right in my throat as if someone had punched me there; the result was going to be positive. She looked extremely happy for me, but that's weird to say or think, since I was only 14 years old – like who'd be happy for a 14 year old kid? Well, she certainly was.

The lady smiled at me, "Congratulations, your test came out positive, you're pregnant!"

There was a bit of a delay before it actually registered in my brain. I looked over at my friend and he looked as if he had seen a ghost. He slowly sat down and said, "I think I'm going to faint and I'm not even the father!" Tristan was one of my good friends. I had called him the day before to tell him that I needed someone to go with me to get a pregnancy test because I missed two months of my period and my soon to be son's dad didn't want to come with me. I didn't trust anybody else but Tristan. I knew that this secret would not have been kept if I had brought a girlfriend along. Girls and their drama was a given at that age and I didn't want to be a victim during this vulnerable time in my life. I had to think ahead, so I asked my most trust worthy guy friend – and no regrets.

My emotions were running deep and high as I sat on the public transit on my way home. I wasn't focused on anything because everything was going through my head. I thought about how I was going to tell *him* – hoping in the back of my mind that maybe this would bring us back together.

Our conversation that evening literally went like this:

Me: "Hi, I'm pregnant!"

Him: "Okay."

However it played out that night, I played myself. He stuck around for a short while, went to a prenatal class with me once. Then he just decided to switch teams on me even after I went down on my knees and begged for him back. Whatever reason he had not to take me back pregnant, only he knows.

It didn't take long for the news of my pregnancy to spread. All of a sudden, friends and family started turning their backs on me. I was so alienated, living the entire summer of 1998 on a lonely island. I was all of a sudden looked at as the bad one to everyone, everyone whom I'd been there for. The same friends who now called me names like *whore* have had one or two abortions themselves. Most friends were a couple of years older than me and they were having sex too.

I didn't get it. Why were they throwing stones at me, as if they never committed a sin, a sin much bigger than mine in comparison? I started to see the ugly side in people. I knew their deepest secrets but they still acted like they were *holier than thou*. I began to understand what hypocrisy meant – I saw it for my own eyes.

I wanted to take on my responsibility; it's a no brainer. I had sex, now I have to face the consequences; 1+1 = 2, simple. People forget I've always had a choice. I didn't have to keep this child and I certainly didn't have to face this cruel society I was living in. I could have just disappeared, delivered the baby and given it up for adoption. I was being penalized for what I thought was the right thing to do. I had the courage to be a mother and to take on a huge responsibility at such an early age; that's something a lot of people can't fathom. The question still lingers, why? I made this choice from my heart that I was going to keep this baby. This was *my* choice and nothing was going change my mind.

The next hurdle I had to overcome was actually telling my parents. I had already been going to prenatal classes myself. I used to come home late, and my mother used to yell at me (back then we didn't have cell phones – you just hoped that we would come through that door) but little did she know I was taking classes to prepare me for my pregnancy. I didn't have the courage to tell my immediate family yet. I was waiting for the right moment.

In the interim, I was already thinking of a game plan. I knew I couldn't go to high school pregnant. It would've been too much for me to handle. The ridicule from others, teachers, and I've made some so called enemies by just being pregnant. Girls were the meanest to me.

I was never the type of person to back down in a fight. I had gotten into a few physical fights prior to my pregnancy just by reason of other girls wanting to test my waters. Going to a regular high school was not an option for me but that didn't mean I ran out of options either. It was at this time where the poem *Footprints* served me. I felt like there was someone, something, a force that guided me from A to B and C – that just lifted me and walked me to the right path. I had already distanced myself from everyone, my own best friends had turned their backs on me, two-faced me, degraded me, everything you can imagine. I was getting threats all day, prank calls day in and day out and hate messages on my family's voicemail. Imagine just entering your freshman year about 4 months pregnant – it's normal for others to think the way they did; but it was still wrong.

I spent the rest of my summer figuring things out. An AHA moment hit me one day and something stood out from the pregnancy clinic that I went to for my test. They had given me a Bible and some pamphlets to take home. I immediately scavenged my room to find that little package. I remember I had to hide it to keep my family from seeing any evidence of my pregnancy. I found it at last, tucked away in my drawer, underneath a pile of other magazines. I grabbed everything and laid it on my bed. I first picked up the Bible and held it close to my chest and took a deep breath. Then I picked up a pamphlet that said *The Massey Center* – it just stood out. I picked it up and read through it. It was perfect for me. They helped young expectant mothers. It was a place where you could live and have your baby and also go to school.

There was someone watching over me and they knew exactly where I needed to go. I immediately picked up the phone and called them. I spoke to a woman and I gave her my story. At first she tried to tell me they were full and they were not taking anyone in at that time. I think when I told her my age, she had a change of heart. She told me that someone would get back to me later in the week.

It didn't take too long to for that someone to call me back; if I can recall, it was the same day. I got accepted, they gave me the date as to when I was able to move in to live there and start school. In less than a month, I was going to go away – how I was going to explain all of it to my parents, I didn't know.

Again, the stars aligned themselves. One late evening a few weeks after I was accepted to stay at the Massey Center, I had gotten to a huge fight with my soon to be child's father. His mind was made up, that no way in hell he was going to be a part of the baby. Even though things were only getting worse between us, I still felt it in the bottom of my heart that in time we were going to get back together for the sake of our unborn child. It was about 1am and I was screaming at him at the top of my lungs. I was hysterical. My mother came down with a worried look on her face. She asked me what was wrong. I yelled back at her, with tears flowing down my face, "I don't care anymore, my life is over!" I bawled.

A look of curiosity on her face, she walked towards me and asked me what I meant by that. Still crying I told her I didn't care anymore, that my life was over and I told her how much I hated "him". She leaned over to me (a mother's intuition) and softly asked me "Why do you say that, are you pregnant?"

This was the moment; the opportunity that I've been waiting for to tell her what was really going on with me. With the phone still in my hand, I hung it up. I cried louder confessing "YES!" and turned the other cheek waiting for her to slap me right across my face. Instead, my mother, calm cool and collected, dropped to her knees and asked me how many months along I was. Then she told me to hang on as she reached for the cordless phone. She called my Aunt Rita long distance and asked her for advice. My auntie Rita told her, my pregnancy was a blessing, that I must keep the baby and not to abort it. That night we all had a family intervention at 2am. I too made it clear to everyone that I was not going to have an abortion, that I was going to give birth, whether I had their support or not – my mind was made up and I'd already fallen in love with my unborn child.

My mother's main concern was my schooling. I confessed to her that I'd been going to prenatal classes and that was the reason why I had been coming home so late the odd times during the week. I also told her that I was leaving in a couple of weeks and that I'd be staying at a place where I could go to high school. It was the only way. She was actually really surprised that I had my ducks lined up in a row. The decision to leave was the best thing I could've done for myself. I was going to be with other women who weren't going to judge me, who were all going through the same thing I was. We only had one mission and it was to become a mother; most importantly it was away from all the negativity. I had to stay out of the spotlight; there was something else much more important growing inside me and I had to do what was best.

Picture that, I'd just survived telling my family the news of my pregnancy, phew. I was ready to leave everything and start this new life. Everyone had turned their backs on me, including the person who meant the most to me. Even my closest cousin told me I'd ruined my life and I was on my own (I didn't hear back from her until years later). There was nothing left to stick around for; I had to keep it moving. The father couldn't handle being ridiculed, and questioned why he would stay with me. Apparently I was just some bitch and he clearly forgot that we were once madly in love; having to accept it was agonizing. Instead he made the decision to join the rest of them and continued to throw stones at me; I guess that's what teenagers do but in my opinion, it was an excuse. He was just a coward.

March 18, 1999 at 13:43, I gave birth to a healthy baby boy. I named him Traehnel Dominiq (which is Heart spelled backwards and 'Nel' from Nelson Mandela and Dominiq is pronounced *dom-min-nic*). He was just perfect, with a cute little button nose; he was a beautiful baby. His eyes sparkled the moment I looked right into them. I knew this child was something special, even the nurses thought so. They kept taking him from me and cuddling him as if he was an angel. Traeh (nickname) was my Angel, a blessing; he's the #1 reason I became the person I am today.

One thing is certain; this child was made from pure love. Now my son is 14 years old and just graduated elementary school from an enriched gifted program because he's a little genius. I would do it over and over again just to be in where I am today.

This was God's love, so pure and so innocent, he was mine to keep. What started out to be a mess in other people's eyes turned out to be nothing but a blessing in my life. I am grateful to have been blessed at such a young age – there are no words to express my gratitude to God for such an amazing life experience and giving me such special boy.

Thinking back now, it felt as if I was living in another life time; my life dramatically changed. I don't know how I managed to overcome that period. We go through so much stress and turbulence in our lives that we forget to breathe and I hadn't realized it until my son was born –I felt a huge weight lift off of my shoulders; almost like a little victory shout "I did it!" I went through pure hell just to have this baby, but it was all worth it in the end and I'd do it all over again and again – all it took was some patience.

Nothing, and I say nothing, in life is ever free. Remember that somewhere out there someone is going through something much worse than you. If you can train yourself to see the bigger picture, you can overcome it. Every situation has a light waiting at the end of every tunnel. Stay strong, everything can be fixed and we've always had that choice. Cuts heal and scars tell stories.

I started with changing the environment I was in and made that choice. Sometimes you just have to remove yourself from everyone or anything that weighs you down. If that's what it takes, cut it off. There's no middle ground, it's either you stay in that dark, dark cloud or you move away from it. The ones who were meant to be in your life will always be there for you.

CHAPTER 3

I think I found love…. It was me.

"So it's not gonna be easy. It's gonna be really hard. We're gonna have to work at this every day, but I want to do that because I want you. I want all of you, forever, you and me, every day…"

Ryan Gosling, The Notebook

We have to move with the essence of time and evolve; we need constant growth within. The more we know about ourselves, our relationships with others start to make more sense. It's about finding the truth, accepting it and making the right choices. It's not our hubby, our BF, co-workers that need the correcting, we have to correct ourselves first – and then we'll start to understand the dynamics of the relationships that surround us.

I always say, pick and choose your battles as long as you have a fair argument. Everyone is different, and everyone has their own way of dealing with situations. If we can see the other person and understand, you will empower yourself because you'll know how to walk away.

There's been so many times that I have had to swallow a lot of my pride when it meant being honest with myself, looking in the mirror and accepting who I am as a person.

We also have to accept the consequences and the responsibility for any bad decisions we've made and then work towards fixing them. We're not perfect. I try not to sit around and wait for someone to feel sorry for me. People will start to feel like you are too clingy and you'll make them feel like you're a responsibility; that's the least you want someone to feel about you – a responsibility. Right before you know it, you'll start to feel desperate and you'll find yourself settling for less, just because it's there.

During another one of my tough times, I was going through what I called a limbo. I was so infatuated and in love with my son's dad (as you all know, it started from day one). When my son was roughly around 3 years old, his dad started coming back into my life; and this time, I thought romantically. I thought maybe this time; we were going to be a family. I had all this emotion bottled up inside me and I couldn't wait to show him happiness. I couldn't wait to be that perfect girlfriend, that perfect woman, the perfect mother to his child. I was living to stay in love with him. My whole existence revolved around being in love and wanting him to love me back and it's fair to say it was an obsession because he never felt the same way about me. If he ever did, I'd never know because he's had a messed up way of making me feel otherwise.

We had different goals in life. We were still fairly young, and although we remained good friends, I could feel that he wasn't as in love with me as I was with him. Even knowing that, I still tried to pursue it.

Trying to maintain a close friendship with the person you're in love with doesn't always work – I learned that the hard way. I've established that everything I did, I did it because of him, and I did it in hopes that he'd come to a realization and see how much he meant to me. Even though at the end of the day it only hurt me – I still didn't care. I felt I deserved the pain.

I was looking for love in all the wrong places and what seems to be with the wrong person, and since he didn't love me I started to look for it elsewhere and put myself in dangerous situations all in the name of 'love'.

For all the bad things that were happening to me I started to blame him, to the point where I was losing myself. I was broken. I didn't eat, I didn't sleep, and I experimented with marijuana and put myself in the worst situations to numb the pain. I made several bad decisions because I didn't care anymore. The last straw for me was when someone took advantage of me. He was much older than me. We were out with some friends and we started drinking. I could've been more responsible but the next thing you know, I was passing in and out, and to this day, I can't really recall what happened but I am alive. I remember when I started to get back my consciousness the first person I thought of was him, not my son, not my mother, not God but him.

I had tears rolling down my eyes, the pain was inevitable. I remember being dropped home. My mom answered the door and I ran to the shower, stumbling on my way up the stairs – but luckily she was oblivious to it all. I didn't even take my clothes off; I turned on the shower and jumped right in. I cried. I tried to cry the pain away; I sat there, with my clothes still on, trying to remove the filthy dirty feeling, like someone took something from you that you know you'll never get back. I remember my last thought before I knocked out in bed. I thought, "If I had his love, this would've never happened."

I forgot who I was. I forgot my goals, my visions, my dreams and I was slowly losing my dignity. As a woman, that was the only thing left in me. Because we remained 'good friends', every time we were together, I felt that hope of finally becoming a family and living happily ever after.

We've all dreamt of the Cinderella story as a child, but Disney lies to you.

I couldn't figure it out. What is love anyway? I thought it meant you forgive, forget and love unconditionally. I grew up with both my parents; Growing up I was taught that you fall in love, get married, have kids and live happily ever after; or once you have a baby, you ought to be a family forever. I felt lied to by my parents, teachers and the Television. The truth started to crumble and my expectations as a young girl started to unfold in the worst way. I was never once taught the honest truth about love and relationships. The mirage started disappearing.

I couldn't imagine not living life any other way – just him, me and our son, happily ever after just like the movies. I felt like he loved me but at the same time, I felt he hated me so much that he resented me. Whatever his defense is, it is what it was. He made me feel really small. I know that I too hurt him but that was the past and I thought maybe he would've already forgiven me, just like I forgave him – wishful thinking I guess but I thought that's what love was all about.

From this, I learned that love is a strong force that comes with every good and bad emotion. There's a thin line and you have to find the middle grounds to feel one with it all.

Questions after questions but no answers. Why couldn't he see that everything I did was for him, everything I was doing was for him? I was raising his son, trying to be the best mother I could be to prove to him that I was the one. There were days I wondered, if I had died that night, would he have acknowledged me? What it would take for him to bake the cake, so I could eat too because it always seemed like he wanted the cake all the time.

What hurt me the most was that he would continuously latch onto people who disliked me, and only wanted nothing but the worst for me. I knew he resented me; the reasons I will never know. I just didn't get it. Truth is he never loved me. I use to cry every night; I forced myself to see the truth. The only feeling I knew was this love for him and I prayed every night for him to love me back, just so he can just feel it for a little bit and be addicted to my love. That was all I had ever known, was that obsession. I felt like that was the real reason for my existence.

I am such a firm believer that God works in mysterious ways, and there's no greater love than God's love. Finally, it seemed like my dream was about to come true. After not giving up on us, he was starting to come around. He was starting to spend time with me and our son. He held my hand, we'd stay up late and we'd put our son to bed together. We were starting to get really close. After years of pretending I thought this was it, it was almost official after sharing a few kisses. We were back talking late night on the phone just like the old days.

No words or colors could express my happiness at that point. I started to see what the future was going to look like – it was heaven and I was on cloud nine. That dream didn't last very long, it all shattered in a blink of an eye.

One day I was at the mall and I happened to bump into him.... and a girl – and not just any girl, they were holding hands. My life flashed before my eyes, I swear I had an out of the body experience. I died that day for a split-second when my heart literally stopped.

I was trembling; I didn't know what to do. I didn't know whether to beat her ass, cry, get into an argument with him, or just faint. Surprisingly, I kept my cool, and let my ego take over. I became cold and I pretended like it never affected me. I became a stranger to him; I became that friend again. I just asked him what he was doing, where he was going and why he was going home with her. That was basically it. I pulled on my big girl panties and left it alone.

The pain I felt that day was unreal; the truth just hits you in the face. No pain will ever compare to that day – ever. They say the truth hurts and it sure as hell does. I think that was the moment I realized what I was doing to myself and my life. I was hopeless and led on. I remember as if I could relive that moment, the anxiety I felt going home. I was on the bus trembling. As soon as I got home, I ran to my bed and cried. I cried like I never cried before. I was lost. I think I was crying more because of how much it had consumed me and that I, nobody else had let it happen. I was ashamed and embarrassed at myself; I was humiliated. No one else was to blame but me.

I had to start over again. I was hurt, broken, my heart ripped out of chest and stabbed. I knew I had to do something about it although I was still in denial. One shoulder was saying he still loves you, one day you'll be together, just wait... and the other shoulder was saying, he doesn't love you, are you blind, it's time to move on.

I never felt the need to approach him. I felt cheated. It was too painful to bring it up to him, even though I wanted answers. I just couldn't. I was a coward; I didn't want to know. So I let it go and moved on with myself. I guess he didn't feel the need to justify anything to me either. We never discussed it, instead we both acted like it never happened. I had to live three years of my life watching this newfound love of his grow from the sidelines. My son would come home and tell me every weekend how much fun he and his dad had along with that individual – during that three year period I was lost and broken.

A piece of poetry I wrote, when I let him go:

Last Look

It tells me too much to look in those infinite eyes

Like a tunnel to your hidden side

What's your flesh trying to hide?

Dissolving when I look through your retina

You are undefined like the colours that they hold

Unable to explain what I see, it just won't unfold

We're the remedy to my soul

So good that we traveled on the same earth plane

Through the solar glaze untamed

Ponderous beats my heart brings

Like death dark songs it sings

I love you, equals the universes belt

It Feels so good but yet it's unfelt

I'd conquer time to prove how much you meant to me

Like a newly created entity, just to love me

Eternally, but I can't this no more emotionally

So if we wake to rewrite these prints

Rearrange the pages of contents

I'll release the energy

No matter how deep it hurts within me

I got you, at the same time, I lost you

Such a snowy blur to find you

I gave up but my soul still needs you

To love you was good and I couldn't get enough

But yet to stay in love with you was tremendously tough

So, I ask the father for my spirit to let you go

As long as darlin' you know

That I loved you deep like the timeless space

Last look into me with love on my face

All things in life open up your eyes and teach you valuable lessons. God knows how much I prayed for him to love me back, and God knows the pain I endured. I asked the Lord that if he wasn't meant to be, "Then show me a sign!" That was the day I prayed for. Almost every day I'd emotionally battle with myself and almost every night I'd ask God to give me a sign. Finally, that day I saw him with another girl, it was clear as day. That was the sign I've been waiting for. I had the answer right in front of my eyes.

After all that, I felt something amazing start to happen to me. I felt like a huge burden that I was carrying was starting to unload. My chest was feeling lighter and I was happy. I cried all the pain away every single night and I woke up every single day feeling like a whole new different person.

"Someone I loved once gave me a box full of darkness. It took me years to understand that this too, was a gift."'

Mary Oliver

That was a blessing in disguise; it really taught me a big huge lesson – to love myself first. If someone doesn't love and respect you like you love and respect that person, no matter how much you love them, you have to let it go, especially when it becomes unhealthy, not just for you but for everyone around you. Coming to grips with reality was very hard to swallow. It felt like I failed my son, which was actually the hardest part of it.

It was at that time I first felt failure. I blamed myself for a lot of things for a while until I understood that this wasn't my fault and this was just a part of my journey. Somehow, there was no other option but to make this work; I was going to do whatever I needed to make it happen for my son and me. It did give me a boost of motivation on the other hand to let out that Go-Getter Honey out of me. When it comes to my children I try not to have any pride or ego. I do whatever it takes even if it hurts me as long as my children are benefitting from it all.

I found a reason for the pain. It really pushed me to push even harder. I finally saw the light! I was going to make something positive out of this experience; it was the end of a chapter. I needed to make something out of myself, so that I don't have to depend on him for anything. That is exactly what I did.

Here I am today, 10 years later. To be honest, I still have a piece of sadness that sometimes lurks through me because I never had the chance to get some answers from that day and I honestly believe we all keep a piece of sadness of some sort. It's what you do with that sadness that makes a difference in your life. You choose how you want to live with it. The only difference now is, I have accepted it as a blessing, and I could have ended up in a much worse situation. We are humans, and it's okay to feel that way as long as you don't let it consume you.

It's easy to change your life and with every decision, there are consequences. I made a wise conscious decision that I was not going to pursue that love anymore; I was ready to live with it. I wanted my son to grow up as normal as can be. He meant everything to me, so I just had to let his dad do what he needed to do.

After that limbo period was dying down, instead of falling apart, I picked up the pieces and put it all back together. It motivated me to do even better and to work even harder. Success is the sweetest revenge and I don't mean this in a bad way (it was a motivation to do better).

Even after the fact, I was good to him as I possibly could be. Instead of showing him I needed him, I bettered myself and showed him that I didn't need him, because it wasn't me that needed him, it was our son and that wasn't going to change. I made sure to keep an amicable relationship with him for my son's sake. I did it by going out and working really hard to get a better job so my son and I could be financially stable. I went out and got my driver's license – young ladies if you want a start to the road of independence, get your driver's license. Trust me, you'll thank me later.

I could've been bitter and used my anger and pain to hurt him, fight, argue, go to courts, and take his rights away as a father. I didn't want a part of that because my son would be the only one who would be affected by it long term. Why would I want to take my son's father away from him? If I can't have him, he can't have him either – that's selfishness. I wanted to work hard so I didn't have to ask him for child support and argue over money and depend on him. To me my son's relationship was far more important than going to court over something material. I'd rather work my butt off and provide for my son and not have to ask him for anything, just as long as he's active in his life. Like I said, when it comes to my children, I have no pride or ego – I try my best to be rational and logical.

I wanted to share that story because I feel like independence is so important – it's like your backbone. When you are stuck in that limbo, and when the limbo really gets you down, you better have a solid back bone to get down low and get back up. Invest time in yourself, doing things you love doing. It's a priceless investment that will be worth a lifetime.

With all that being said, I've lived and I've learned. Now, in a relationship, you move one step up and I'll move one step up. If a guy didn't feel the same way I did, nor invest their time in me, I didn't either. You show me and I'll show you, 50/50 split down to the middle, the feelings should always be mutual. I don't waste any time playing games anymore. I know that persistence pays off, but there's persistence and there's will -- you can't push something that clearly won't budge.

CHAPTER 4

When Friends Fail

"An insincere and evil friend is more to be feared than a wild beast; a wild beast may wound your body, but an evil friend will wound your mind."

Buddha

When friends fail, it's a terrible feeling. I know that we've all been let down by the people we've once upon a time called our sisters, BFF, best friend – happily ever after.

Well, I've had my fair share of losing friends and later realized after a few failed friendships, it was for my own good. It's like something that just hovers over me and gets rid of that bad energy.

I'm not saying I'm holier than thou. I too played both sides of the coin when I was young.

I was once a bully too. I bossed around my friends, treated them with no respect and I didn't care about their feelings. I was young and stupid. Making friends was really easy for me so I took it for granted. Until you face a time in your life when you have nobody, you then realize how you've made people feel. I had some really good people around me but I used to look down on them and thought I was better than them; I was the popular kid, and nobody else mattered. I was responsible for hurting a lot of people's feelings throughout my early childhood. I hurt them because I was then very selfish. I'm not sure where this personality came from. I grew up with the most selfless parents ever or maybe that's it. I always thought my parents used to put their friends first and catered to them more than to me and my sibling's needs. Looking back at it, I think that's why I didn't care much about treating my friends with respect; because my parents didn't give me that attention and I was probably envious of it deep down inside. I've always had a gift of being a seer, and I used it the wrong way. I saw people's weakness and used it to manipulate and hurt them; I've hurt a lot of people's confidence that way which affected them in the long term.

One of my neighbors never had friends to begin with. She wore big thick glasses, had ginger hair and freckles. My friends and I used to tease her, pick on her and pretty much bully her. Whenever we'd see her in the sidewalk, we'd interrogate her and I think maybe once pushed her around; believe me, it hurts me to look back at myself knowing the kind of pain I might have caused her. For all I knew, she could be having some major trouble at home that we weren't aware of. Years later, I met up with my other friend (who also took part in the bullying) and she told me that she bumped into our neighbor. Our neighbor didn't hesitate to tell her how much we've made her life a living hell and that she still has the feelings locked inside her and it's made her into a person full of anger. I didn't like hearing that at all. I would never want people to remember me like I'm some type of monster; it's pretty sad because when I heard that, I knew exactly what she meant. You will never understand the hurt and pain you cause someone until it's happened to you; it's never a good feeling. I've learned to be kind to everyone because you don't know what kind of personal troubles they're going through

I was young and dumb and selfish and I can go on and on. All I know is my intentions have only been pure and it was never intended to hurt anyone. I was too caught up within myself.

When I love, I love hard, I care hard and I always have good intentions and it comes straight from my heart. Everything I do it comes from sincerity. I will even find it hard to say I miss you; if I don't really mean it and feel it from the heart, you won't hear it from me.

I only want to motivate my friends and share my happiness with them and lift them up with me. You can't be fully successful if you don't share it with others. But, I've learned there's a few type of people out there – three types in particular – who give me that anxious feeling that just screams "DANGER", red lights flashing everywhere.

The first type acts like they're forever holy, constantly talking about their belief in God to cover their sins and to keep the skeletons from coming out their closet. They talk about giving back and wanting to save the universe but their actions are opposite from what they tell you – I call this one the Hypocrite.

The second type include the ones who pretend to be your best friend, but for some reason, they always make up excuses not to come to your kid's party, events, social gatherings and so on. They stay on the phone as a shoulder to cry on but they just want to know your weaknesses and all the so-called bad things that are happening in your life. They get some sort of self-gratification from it because they're envious. Or, they talk to you about their problems for hours but won't listen – not even for a minute about yours – I call this one the Jealous Self-Centered Type.

Not least but last, the friend that always has something negative to say. Everything is negative, everything is impossible – but they're perfect. I call this one LOST. I've had my fair share of the three to the point that my body starts having a bad reaction from a mile away. Seriously, I start to get sick.

I remember one situation where a once upon a time friend really hurt me. She had gotten kicked out of her house and needed a place to stay, so of course I let her stay with me at my parent's place. We were teenagers, so we did everything together, told each other our deepest secrets – I really trusted her.

I was dating a guy; we weren't serious but he made me feel good about myself. He always came by to check on me, bought me gifts. He made that extra effort to show me how much he really was into me. One day, things started getting really strange; I just felt it at the pit of my stomach. I had introduced my friend to this boyfriend. I had no idea what transpired, how it transpired, when it transpired and how they exchanged numbers but it happened – behind my back of course. To make a long story short, she told me one day that she was sleeping with my boyfriend (that AHA moment , when your intuition was right), then all of a sudden, started talking bad about me and never came back to my house. So basically, she was sleeping with my boyfriend while she was sleeping under my roof. How classless is that? It's just not right, and it was hurtful because they both started ganging up on me – like I deserved it, like I did something so tragic to them both, when all I did was let her stay at my house. To this day, I am still clueless as to what I did to the both of them for them to cause me so much pain because as far as I know, I was the one who got the shitty end of the stick. I'd say she was the lost and envious type; she covered up her own guilt by making me look like the bad person. It took me until I'd reached adulthood to understand that and I can't get mad for what she did to me simply because I have accepted the fact that someone who's insecure and isn't happy within themselves will always try to blame other people for their actions. The only thing left to do is to stay away, so how can you really be mad at that? You have to learn to forgive those because they don't know any better. It's an emotion you don't want to carry anyway.

The question is, why do friends do the most hurtful things to the ones that care and help them the most? It's jealousy. Jealousy amongst friends is so strong and present and it's always the cause of a bad friendship break-up. Sure, I could've reacted irrationally, and fought them both back and defended myself but I felt I didn't need to. Why am I going to defend myself? What did I have to prove to the both of them, that I was her best friend and he was my boyfriend and we belong together... heck no! The truth is in my face, now what am I going to do with it?

That was the first time I learned the saying "pick and choose your battles" and this was a battle I did not want to fight. It was the hardest thing I had to go through during that time. She was airing out my dirty laundry and he was doing the same.

Sad to say, I think a lot of women have similar stories to mine. I know I'm not the only one. We've all been through situations where we've felt we've been there for somebody, trusted them with practically our entire life but they do nothing but fail you.

From my experience, relationships teach us all valuable lessons and every lesson learned is an experience that makes us into who we are now. We have to change not only the way we approach certain situations but change our perception and reaction. You know what they say, and trust me I live by this – silence is deadlier than any weapon. I must agree with this one. Sounds really messed up, especially if you've had a friend sleep with your boyfriend and now you ought to say nothing?!? Yup, that's right – zip! The law of the universe works better when you don't say anything at all. This law also falls under Patience.

Einstein has gotten the formula down pat, in one of his famous success quotes he simply breaks it down:

If A equals success, then the formula is A equals X plus Y and Z, with X being work, Y play, and Z keeping your mouth shut.

Success doesn't mean just success in life or your career, it works for our well being as well.

Through my teens because of my unique situation of being such an extremely young mom, I went through the drama, the harsh name calling, he said, she said, finger pointing crap. And I figured it out, when I kept my mouth shut and stuck with my confidence, I found they eventually backed off and everything just fell into place. Patience and suppressing my ego played a strong role in it too.

I remember one time I was so hurt. One of my best friends, someone who I admired so much, backed stabbed me left right and center, anywhere she could. I always end up in the middle. I introduce one friend to another friend and next thing you know they're gossiping about me. This girl, I will call her Kelly, was a childhood friend. I had introduced her to another friend of mine, I'll call her Stephanie. They'd probably only been introduced once or twice and we all seemed to get along. Kelly and I had a mutual guy friend, and they were fooling around but not officially, since I also knew she was with someone else. Anyway, my other friend Stephanie was hanging out one day with the same mutual guy friend. She fell for him right off the bat and I guess he liked her too (or maybe he was just a womanizer).

One thing led to another and they slept together the same night. Okay, what am I supposed to do, what's done is done. We're all young adults and I don't see why I should be lecturing Stephanie – if she wanted to sleep with him, she could decide that herself. To fast forward the story, Kelly and Stephanie found out on their own that they had slept with the same guy and decided to blame me. So they both ganged up on me, calling me a bad friend. They made me feel like shit to be honest because I almost believed them. Then the lies started spreading, and of course it would hit the people closest to me that I cared about. They tried to ruin me by gossiping my secrets to the world (yes we all have skeletons in our closets). I was so hurt at this point I literally just wanted to kill myself. The constant harassment was unbearable. I was being bullied. I get it; Kelly felt it was my responsibility to tell Stephanie that they had slept together. I have to disagree with both. You make your bed you lie in it. I saw why they were really upset; it wasn't because of me, they were mad at themselves and the decision they made to sleep with the guy. So blame it on the girl who didn't sleep with him, right?

It got so bad at one point that I almost started believing the things they were saying about me. It's all nonsense. That's what people want from you. They will project their insecurities and their misery onto you; they get the satisfaction of knowing you're feeling their negative energy. Old saying that never gets old: "Misery loves company".

Through it all, I took their drama. I fought back to defend myself, but that only got me so far. Drama is exhausting. I eventually just left it behind and stayed quiet. I was no longer going to entertain it. I was done.

After a lot of patience and by using the self-discipline not to react, it started to all fade away. "Aha!" I thought to myself "Duh! If I fuel the fire, it only gets bigger." I realized that by not entertaining such nonsense, sticking to my truth and knowing my intention wasn't to hurt anyone, I was setting myself free.

I call these types of friends Vampires and Leeches; they will suck and steal your energy, leaving you frail and brittle. This is when Karma strikes, because energy is more alive than what we think. You steal someone's energy that doesn't belong to you, it will go back to its home and when it leaves you, Karma is born. Think about it.

It was tough having to deal with the drama alone. During that time I was going through some turmoil with my son's dad, so I was on the brink of losing it – but nobody knew because I kept it all inside; I was known for that hard exterior but I was really like butter inside, slowly melting.

I was trying to figure myself out and raise a young son while everyone else had no responsibilities. I had to balance being a teenager and a mother. That loneliness was dark and cold, and every night I would pray to God to send me a real friend, just one that could take the loneliness and pain away – someone who wouldn't judge me, sometime who would understand me. I remember I used to admire people who had a circle of friends but at the same time I didn't envy them because I knew about the gossiping amongst each other that goes on. At times I used to think, maybe there was something wrong with me, or maybe I should learn to ignore the negative things; I used to question how others did it.

Either way, I was alone at that time of my life. When I say I had nobody, I had nobody. I had no real friends; thank God for my son because he filled that void and kept me grounded. It didn't feel the same, but it was like food; the love in his eyes it kept me alive inside.

I didn't think I was normal at all; I wasn't like all the other kids. For every hurdle I endured, it was 100 times heavier than with average girls at my age. Deep down my intuition was signaling me that being in an unhealthy friendship, I wasn't being a good mother. I was poisoning myself and wasting valuable time while my son needed me. Being a good mother was all that mattered during that cold and lonely time I was alone. It was always my priority, and anything that got in the way of that, I had to re-evaluate and make changes. Remember, as a mother, or even as a woman, what you absorb affects your family, your home and your well-being. Protect your space as it is your sanctuary; you need to feel peace, serenity and positivity always. Your space affects your well- being.

We have to stop denying this feeling; I'd describe it as that uneasy feeling right in the pit of your stomach that sometimes makes you feel nauseous. If it doesn't jibe and you're losing sleep over it, walk away from it and don't look back or try to figure it out.

I'm at this point in my life now where I can't turn the other cheek and fake it (geez, I can hardly fake an orgasm) and contin-ue to maintain fake friendships. This doesn't mean you have to start burning bridges because you dislike everyone and every-thing; you can do this by finding solitude and distancing yourself from the nonsense without burning bridges. The key is to not hurt people with our decisions. This can be done, if you just walk away and do your own thing. If you're not healthy for me and your intentions aren't pure, then there's no stopping by to play, I will just go on my merry way. It's obvious to me now that there are only certain people who will help you grow and bring out the best in you. They are the ones worth your time and energy. I have lived and gained enough wisdom to know exactly what I want in my friendships.

It took me years to understand and realize where I stand as a friend. I've had the pleasure of bumping into a couple of child-hood schoolmates and the first thing I did was to apologize for my actions and behavior; "Sorry" was the first thing that came out my mouth after not seeing them for over a decade. Maybe it was my Karma to be let down and hurt so many times after all, so I can feel the abandonment, hurt and pain. It's not hard to do the math – you're mean to people, you'll get the same treat-ment right back. You'll eventually meet your match. My mother has always told me, what you do to people, will go right back to your children. It would break my heart to know if my children were being picked on and treated like an outcast. So I make the conscious effort to be always kind.

This is where I came to the understanding that my actions cause a chain reaction. That feeling of being bullied and betrayed, I wouldn't wish that on others; especially on my very own chil-dren. It's elementary, the motto that never gets old: Treat oth-ers the way you'd like to be treated.

After a few situations with my so-called friends and feeling what it's actually like to be bullied I had to get rid of the chip on my shoulder. I began to sympathize more with others and try to always give them the benefit of the doubt until they proved me otherwise. It took a few tears and hurtful years to become the friend I am now, but I'm happy and confident of who I came out to be after numerous dark clouds.

I had two options, either be a mean and a vindictive person and try to get back at the world or show the world what we lack: compassion. I chose to be the compassionate one.

My advice to live by – don't seek revenge, don't keep hatred but only love in your heart and learn to forgive others and yourself. Life is a learning process; we find answers in our experiences and gain wisdom. With that I end the chapter by thanking my old friends for teaching me how to take care of the friends in my life today and how to value real friendships. I wish you all nothing but love and happiness in our journey. The Karma ends here.

CHAPTER 5

Mother Me

"Tell the children the truth."

Bob Marley

It's just human nature, I truly believe. Women are born with this maternal gift should we choose to have children. Once a woman becomes pregnant, we're prepping for motherhood already and we don't even realize it.

For example, while pregnant during the last trimester we often find ourselves going to the bathroom in wee hours of the night. I would just get up from my sleep without feeling as groggy as I would when I'm not pregnant. I'd wake up about 3-5 times in the evening depending on how much I had to drink. I've made a connection with post pregnancy when we have to get up at night because the baby is hungry and needs to be fed. Women may come from different lifestyles but when we become a mother, we begin to tap into the universal energy of motherhood. From not being able to wake up, to being trained naturally by your instinct to get up every 2-3 hours to feed your baby, to me this should be considered one of the beauties in life of being a woman, that our bodies just know when and how to adjust.

Being so young, I wasn't educated enough about becoming a

mother and having children when my first son was born. I really didn't have any expectations. I took it one day at a time and I relied on just going with my gut instincts on what was right and following my maternal intuition.

There's been many times when the midwives, nurses and even doctors would tell me what to do and how to do it but I'd often disagree. One example, I had a friend of mine who was the type to try to always go by the book. One day her child started getting rashes on her face and she took her to the doctors. The doctor prescribed a cream as he said it was only eczema and it would go away within 5-7 days and to come back then. During the 5-7 days the rashes started to worsen, spreading all through the child's body. During this time, the parent still took the doctor's advice and kept putting the prescribed cream. The rash had gotten so severe and still – they waited it out. After the 7 days, they went back to the doctors and the doctor was shocked to see how bad the rashes had gotten and how much it had spread that he even asked "Why didn't you take her to emergency?" Come to find out the child had developed some sort of Herpes rash (which I later found this was actually common in kids) and they can get it anywhere. I'm not saying do not listen to what the doctor has to say but you have to also listen to that gut feeling when you look at your child and something inside you says, "This doesn't seem right". There's nothing wrong with challenging the doctor's diagnosis, they're humans too and often make mistakes, it happens all the time. I'm just showing you, that this intuition has always been around and it has always been there – so why not tap into it and exercise it? When it comes to my children, I don't risk it. Remember that old saying "Mothers know best"? – Well it's because we do.

Many people would give me advice about parenting and they don't have children themselves. It's cute. It almost sounds as if they just read a "How to be a mom 101" book. I'd sit there and listen but if it didn't jibe with me, then I'd take my own intuition into consideration first before I'd take theirs. That's how I've kind of Stevie Wondered my way as a young mom. I knew what worked and I knew what didn't and that also takes paying close attention to your child and observing their uniqueness. I'm not a by the book mom that's for sure, more like follow my maternal intuition mom – because I don't really believe there's one standard way of parenting children. All kids and babies are different. We are in a society where we are culturally diverse and don't always share the same values; if anything we should be the ones to adjust ourselves to our children. Children are all unique.

The last parent/teacher interview I went to, the teacher told me that my son (then three) needed to learn to take school seriously. I looked at her dumbfounded and in my head I thought, "He's three!" I'm not too thrilled about what she said. If I told my son to take school seriously, I don't think he'd even comprehend that. Children are so unique and different, I think the intelligent thing to do is to take the time to observe the child and figure out what works and what doesn't with them. Children are sensitive to emotion, more so than adults. If teachers learned to tap into a child emotionally, they will learn to behave and listen to them. Instead of putting down a child, boost their confidence, make them feel better about themselves and they will respect you in return. They will attach that feeling of goodness to you and they'll learn to trust you. I find for the last 14 years – during my eldest son's lifetime – most teachers focused on the bad. Oh your child can't pay attention, here's the doctor. Oh your child has dyslexia only to find out later in life that same very child becomes a world class athlete.

We all have a soul and a purpose and it goes deeper than just a diaper change. What we should focus on is nurturing our children to be become the person they're meant to be.

Taking care of my eldest son wasn't that hard – I'd say it was a walk in the park. That's right a walk in the park! It was having to balance my life that was the most challenging part. I was just a child, with a child, now how do you balance that?

I wasn't angry or sad and I didn't have any regrets about my choice to be a young mother. Instead I embraced it – that's one load off my back. I loved being a mother and I still enjoy every minute of it. My son wasn't your average baby/kid either. I knew that this kid was gifted and knowing that, I nurtured his gifts and curiosity.

That's the difference between me then and me now. I was young and I didn't have any responsibilities but to take care of my son and go to high school – two things literally. I didn't really care about anything else or care to hang out with friends – that wasn't my top my priority and it was by choice. I remember after school, I'd have to rush home to pick up my son from the babysitter's and my boobs used to be so engorged that I had to pump in the girl's bathroom before I left school – I had about an hour and a half commute. All I could think of was how much he must be missing me and I couldn't wait to breastfeed him because my boobs were hurting like you would've never imagined. I didn't like the fact that someone else was watching him. Instead of wanting to hang out at subway stations and malls after school, I rushed home to be with my son; I'd rather be at home with him. I enjoyed teaching him and nurturing him.

Having so many more responsibilities now in life – it feels like there's just not enough time in the day. Sometimes, we must do what we have to do and keep on going. It's like taking it back into the days when we didn't rely on technology and the hours of the day seemed longer; we kept ourselves busy with life. I'm guilty of not having the same amount of time I put in my first child with my two youngest and very much aware of it but I try to balance it out the best I can. I'm a working mother and I know like most working parents would love to have more time with our children but we have to work to provide for the very same children. When we get home from work, it's dinner, and then we have to clean up and get them ready for bed, not to mention if your kids are into extracurricular activities, that'll take up more time in between.

The challenge is, where in the world do I find that same quality time that I did with the first? Well, I just do and I don't think about it – it's got to work. Every time you're with your child it's an opportunity to bond and get to know them. Whether we're at the doctor's office or driving home, I pick their brains. It's important to know your child and what they're strengths and weaknesses are and it's our job to nurture that. There are times where, you know what, I'd rather order take-out so I can cut down on prepping time so that we can have more family time. Sometimes that's two extra hours – it's worth it.

Anytime kids ask you questions, that is the most opportune time to educate them and to talk to them – so I try to be as honest as I possibly can. You still want them to enjoy their youthful, innocent minds and not poison them with society's expectations. I learn so much about myself and new things in life just by listening to or answering their questions. This also helps me to figure out their personalities and it's much easier to parent them and cater to them. One is highly sensitive, so I always have to put extra time nurturing his emotions and explaining why he got into trouble. One is tougher in the outer shell but like dough in the inner shell; always holding their feelings inside. This one I don't do much explaining because they get it, they just need to always feel loved and that's how they forget. It's important so they don't hold any negative emotions inside since they're the type of kid that holds their feelings in. You want to try to never leave your kids with a negative emotion. The other one is very much like my own image (oh boy) but the alpha male, this is the one I have the most challenging time with because our energies bounce off each other − the positive part about it is we learn so much about ourselves in terms of inner growth, a negative + a negative = a positive. He acts as my back bone. I remember once, I was so upset with my eldest child (who's more like me) and we were driving home. I yelled at him and asked him if he had any common sense at all. He replied "No, mom common sense doesn't exist, it's the common way people think and I don't think like common people." I literally had to bite my tongue, shut down and think hard about what he'd just said. How could I argue with that? Instead, I respected his answer and tried to work with him. It's obvious that he doesn't think like me or most people, so from then on, I put that extra effort to get where he's coming from. I tell you it's not easy but with understanding and patience, it helps with parenting. These are

young souls who once lived here and are now in a new world –
think about it, wouldn't you be curious too?

I take full credit for raising my eldest son to a great genius kid
(wink) – no he's not perfect but I make sure he has a good
head on his shoulders. From the day he was born I knew he
was special. There was something about this kid, and his eyes
looked like an old wise soul. When I lived at the Massey Center,
I spent the majority of my time bonding with my unborn child.
I remember my mother said to me while pregnant with Traeh
that there used to be an old study where a child came out as
a genius but both parents had average IQ's. They asked the
mother what she did differently in her pregnancy, routine and
diet. She said that she had taught her unborn child while in the
stomach. She'd read to her stomach, played music and kept
a positive mind. So my mother told me to do the same thing.
I'm not sure if there's been an intense study on this topic but I
know it to be true. Maybe they can see once the fetus brain has
been developed, how it reacts to noise and the connection to
its mother when she's sad, angry, happy through her emotions.
I'm not a doctor but anyhow, if you want another example, read
up on Pavarotti, he's one of the top tenors. His mother only
played opera music throughout her pregnancy and he became
one of the world's best tenors. Back to the story, so for the first
time I actually took my mother's advice and she was right – are
you surprised, mothers are always right! He started talking and
walking at nine months and by the time he was only one he was
talking better than most three or four year olds – people would
be shocked and they'd ask me how old he was the time. My son
was labeled as gifted in his school board when he was in the 5th
grade. Since then he's been taking enriched programs, and as of

the 7th grade, he got in to an enriched program that was taught in a high school. I'm proud of how he turned out especially because people looked down on me and my son. Just because I taught him in my stomach that doesn't mean the nurturing ends there. From the day they're born, your emotional and spiritual responsibility to the child is to give them love and security. Kids have to feel that for as long as they can remember – especially during the early stages. Building their confidence is very important.

I myself am also a firm believer in breastfeeding your baby. I breastfed all three of my children and the longest I've nursed one was until he was about five. I know I'll get criticized about that but back home it's not something that's foreign, so why should I be ashamed? I think our media connects the female body to sexuality and that's where I think the problem is. I don't believe in disconnecting from your child at an early stage either. I know a lot of people who put their kids – a newborn in a new big nursery right after they come home from the hospital. Think about it – from the womb to the room. Again, I'm not any kind of pediatrician or child psychologist but from my experience as a mother and being spiritually aware at the age of six months; the feeling of security and love is the only thing a child that small should feel. They have to feel that security; when you leave them in a cold big room in this crib in the dark, wouldn't you feel the loneliness and abandonment?

My sister and I were pregnant at the same time, how bizarre. My son is one month and ten days older than my niece. My sister and I weren't really close but being pregnant together brought us closer. I don't think I ever really looked up to my sister, I just liked her clothes. I did always wanted to have a sister to kind of have my back that was the only expectation I had from her, especially during the days of having to deal with jealous girls and their drama but she never came through for me. Nonetheless, our little guys practically grew up together from the womb.

Here's a question for all women out there, if you had to choose between your first love and your child, which of your heart's possession would you give up?

My sister was living common-law with her boyfriend when she had a baby girl but unfortunately it didn't work out. So my sister moved back in with my parents with her daughter and at that time I was still living at home too. We were one big happy family again. I was pretty happy that my sister moved back home. She was my best friend at the time and I enjoyed having her and my niece around and this time we had something in common – we were both mothers. She did go through a rebellious stage where she was out every night with friends because she felt she was suppressed in her last relationship for too long, playing a role of being in love with someone when her mind and was with somebody else. Of course, I didn't mind taking care of my niece while she was clinking glasses at 2 am. It felt like I had two kids – at 16. That being said, she reconnected with her first love. He happened to be single, living in L.A. He would fly up to see her often enough to see that it was obvious, they were back together again – reunited! There's a cost for that. It was her daughter, my niece. I never really knew that this kind of love existed, strong and blinding enough that you'd pick a man over your very own daughter. My sister gave up my niece so that she could be with her soul mate. Literally signed her rights away to her ex, the girl's father.

I didn't get this at all. Here I am, I chose a life to become a young mother and there she is – she just throws in the towel and says she doesn't want to do this anymore. Was it really that easy to just change your mind like that? "Oh hey, I don't want to be a mother to her anymore, sign here." I couldn't believe my sister did that. So here I was taking care of my niece. Not only did I have to work out a schedule with my son but I was working out a schedule to see my niece. There were those nights where this two year old girl would look me in the eye and ask me if her mom was still at work – it had already been months since she'd left. I just didn't have the heart to tell her that her mom was gone, or I did but I knew she wouldn't understand. My niece would stay up late, waiting for her mom because she didn't know she left, she'd sniff her blanket for her mother's scent and fall asleep waiting for her mom to come home.

The pain in my heart that my sister caused over her selfish decision just opened my eyes in a way unimaginable. Again, the ugly side of life started sinking in, all these emotions were new to me and again I thought deeper into things so I could try to make sense of it all. Children are the most vulnerable and I started to see how this can unfold when a child has to go through trauma in their childhood. I had to be there for my niece, there was no other choice. She became my priority. I weighed in the pros and cons, what if I just left it alone between my sister and her ex and I'll just live my life. I couldn't do it, I couldn't just move on without her. Her mother abandoned her and I wasn't going to do the same. I took a lot of crap by trying to stay in my niece's life. Her father didn't want anything to do with my family and refused to let us see her for three years. Until, I finally got fed up trying to fight her father with no power of authority whatsoever. Something had to be done and I called my sister to come back to fight for her. I stuck by my sister's side throughout the entire custody battle –she won joint custody and got back half of her rights. The pieces were starting to slowly come to together. I now had a routine to see my niece and I vowed to her I would never miss it. Those nights waiting for the cops to come get my niece, we'd wait inside our car in the blizzard for hours while my four year old niece would constantly look out the window to see if we were still outside because her father wouldn't let me see her regardless of the court order. The time I had to deal with CAS and put my own children at risk. It was all worth the battle. I'd rather sleep for the days of my life not wondering what my niece is doing but rather knowing how she is doing.

If you are committed to make things better, there's no giving up. From the time you make that commitment, there was a vision that went along with it as well. The universe transpires to clear your path once you think of something with pure intention – but it doesn't happen overnight. All you have to do is stay committed to that ideal. I dealt with Children's Aid for years, putting my own family into jeopardy. I took all the punches from her ex, the emotional beating, custody battles -- I picked up all her drama. My niece was something special and my heart couldn't just give up on her. I asked the Lord, "Why me?" Well, I don't know the answer to that but it has made me an even stronger individual for my own children.

It's funny how things in life happen, even though my son's dad and I were in good terms and I didn't choose a path of custodial battles, I still lived to go through it. So I know what it's like and trust me, it's not a healthy road to take. My advice would be to be as amicable as you possible can with the opposing party before it gets ugly. Swallowing your pride when it comes to your children and defeating an ego that only wants to dominate is empowering. Living harmoniously is the way to go; you have to learn to be in harmony with yourself first. This is why I had to weigh the pros and the cons; had I made the opposite choice, I wouldn't be living harmoniously because in the back of my mind, I wouldn't be at peace within myself having known I could've done much more.

Think first, instead of acting out irrationally, because all our choices affect us one way or the other. I always say, if you can't scratch the surface you have to look underneath. Peace and harmony within you is good mental health.

Having to see the pain that my sister had caused everyone just made me realize how important kids are to our future. Think about it, the children are our future and they have the power to either cause destruction or create peace in the world – and this starts with home and family. I had set up my life to go as smoothly as possible with my son's dad and his family because I didn't believe in the court system. I took punches from his family too but you know what, I learned to understand why they behaved that way towards me in the beginning. You can't get mad at people who don't know any better – and this is a golden rule for yourself as well. I love my son too much to let my ego get in the way. Egos create fear; it's the one thing that blocks the positive energy from cleansing your mind and soul. As long as you put your ego aside in appropriate situations, everything just falls into place for the better. You're not making decisions that only affect you now; it has more of an effect on your children.

I've had friends, distant and close who always let their ego direct them and they don't see how much it affects their child. Don't ever choose money over your child and get caught up in chasing child support. Here's my outlook on being once upon a time a single mother:

- Try to keep a calm and collective relationship with your child's mother/father, that's number one,

- Number two is, if they can't pay child support, don't chase them. Let it be your motivation to want to do better, work extra hard to fill in the gap.

So yes, be independent and have something going for yourself; if the significant other is someone you can't depend on, cut the grief and learn to depend on you.

I never really understood when two people break up and all of a sudden the man has to take care of their exes and their money wasting lifestyle. I think the obligation to you should be cut off but not his obligation to the child. I've seen it happen where a friend was entirely living off her ex – no job, nothing going for them. Then they ask me why life is so hard? Yes, life is hard for all, why make it harder for yourself? If money is stressing them, then go out and get job, a hobby, go get happy.

Also speaking as a woman, it's in us, it is in our nature to provide, protect and shelter our offspring – look at mother robin. I love it when we are at our natural intuitive state and there's nothing like a mother's intuition. I don't think a book on parenting can really give you a certificate with a big green PASS on it. Our maternal intuitions do. We're just built to adapt to our kids, the connection has always been there. Remember, a soul picked you to be their mother/father here in this lifetime! the connection was already made before they are born. They saw something special in you that they could learn from in this lifetime.

Negative emotions stem from the EGO – fear, guilt, jealousy, insecurity – so try to practice a healthy mind. I say this because we're the first person our children sees as a hero. My mother has always told me, that once you have a kid, you have to be mindful of how you treat others because it's not just your Karma anymore but it'll go to your children first. You reap what you sow.

CHAPTER 6

Go Get It

"If there is no price to be paid, it is also not of value."

Albert Einstein

Growing up my mother always told me, "You should be a lawyer!" She ties that little fierce attitude of mine to those female prosecutors on crime shows she watches on television religiously. A mother always knows best, well not quite. I didn't become that lawyer she hoped for me to become but I did gain a quality which lawyers have and that's being able to reason. That is (music please) to be a strong minded individual, in total control of her thoughts and with the freedom of will to be whoever I want to become.

Since I was a child I've always been a great observer, I believe that's one of the reasons why I have a no games/ no patience attitude. I think it's a gift to be able to see things for what they are. I find that a lot of women are afraid to see things for the way they are. I like being the Batman not the Robin; I wasn't always the best at being the sidekick because I can negotiate for myself. I know from past experience people will respect you for that. I do feel like I'm a natural born leader; however that doesn't mean I know everything. Leaders create other leaders.

I've been told I'm a very opinionated and vocal person and oftentimes I get mistreated or misunderstood. I'm different; I had no choice but to be this way. I had to protect myself from cruel people but most of all I am my own worst enemy. I'm never content when it comes to chasing dreams. We're all different, and I've always like excitement, something to look forward to and once I achieve a goal, it's hard to stop there. It works both as my weakness and my strength, but most of the time it serves me well.

In my later teens, after having to go through various emotional rollercoasters, I got tired, not physically tired but I was mentally and emotionally tired of just riding along the road of life with no sense of direction. I needed something better for my son and I've always been a confident person but this time I had to use this confidence as fuel to go out and get it. What's being confident if you have nothing going for you?

I started dreaming again, rebuilding the pieces of my childhood dreams... but not just dreaming, I also started to live as if I was already there. Every day I woke up, I kept my eyes on the prize and my mentality was always getting there. I knew what I needed to do to get close to it.

At this point in my life, I discovered who I was. I was already a mother of a 4 year old at 18, and I'd seen almost everything, but now what? I couldn't just waste life – I survived it. I wanted things out of life now and I needed change. I felt I had paid my dues to society, and now it's my turn. I wanted a corporate job, a family, a new car, a house, you know the normal things you dream of as a child, although these were things that were impossible for me to have at the time. I knew I could go get it if I wanted too – what's stopping me, a baby? Absolutely not. That was what everyone expected from me – a failure, just a single teenage mother who's going to be nothing; I've heard it all before.

To me, I meant so much more than what they saw me as. I had to be the perfect role model for my son. I had to start a solid foundation. One day, something came over me and I started to write everything down on a paper, wrote a timeline describing when I would like achieve my goals. This is a perfect example of one of the popular universal laws – The Law of Attraction. I didn't know much about it at that time but all I knew was I had the desire, the fiery thing inside called passion. Now, getting there wasn't anything like a walk in the park. This was a new chapter I had to face and just like the old, I'd have to go through the bullshit first – nothing is ever free. Life had already thickened my skin to be ready for this.

I remember going to the employment office where you can go to get help finding jobs and work on your resume – it was government funded and anyone can go. I had no real background except for helping my sister with filing because her BF at the time owned his own business. I also worked part-time at a local burger joint when I was in the eighth grade (I'll elaborate more on that after). Those were the only two experiences I had under my belt. I dropped out of high school so I needed to do something. I remember walking around the mall, handing out resumes, hoping someone would call me. I only had two options, be optimistic or be pessimistic. That was the battle I had in my head almost every day when I wanted to give up. But giving up was way too easy – getting there was a lot more challenging.

I was more determined than ever. I had to take the negative and make it into something positive. I was at this point where I needed to make some sort of income. My parents were struggling and I didn't want to become a burden. Every day I pushed and motivated myself to get out there and look for something. My perception started changing and everything became an opportunity. After months of hard work, failed interviews, getting sprayed by the bus in the rain, going to an interview soaking wet, I still stayed positive. My mother didn't push me to do this, I wanted to push myself. There's nobody else that's going to do it for you or push you to do something but yourself.

This brings me to my first job ever that I mentioned earlier. It wasn't much of a job. I was just paid under the table to help out. I was only in the 8th grade (I've always thought working was cool – I must have gotten that from my parents, because that's all they do/did). I wanted to share this story because even though it was "nothing" I made it into something. It was at a neighborhood burger joint and I was getting paid $6 per hour for two hours on Fridays during the lunch rush in the summer. My friends would come in to order their fries and gravy ('til this day I will still visit that burger joint just to feel nostalgic) and see me there. I wasn't ashamed even though some of the kids would make little comments. I felt good about myself. I looked at the big picture; I was one step ahead of my friends at the time. They didn't know I was making only $12 for the day, so I made it seem like I was making $30 ($30 was a big deal when you're 14). I wasn't going to be made fun of – I had the confidence to be a leader and I had to believe I was leading by example. I had to make it look like what I was doing was a cool thing by being proud of it. I felt grown and independent. That feeling stayed with me for a long time – it felt good to be that independent young lady who made her own money. That was one of the first times I felt that and it was all coming back to me.

Resume after resume, I landed my first retail job at a shoe store (that didn't last long). I felt like I was a big shot, seriously. I was one of "them". I'm now part of the working class, so nobody can tell me anything. I can buy things for my boy with my own money and I'm doing something with my life. I was getting paid anywhere between $6 per hour to $ 11 per hour. I always made sure that I was never running on empty and kept my foot on the pedal. I didn't care what I was making, as long as I knew why I was doing it and where I was going. Particularly speaking in the workplace; I've seen many women who tend to get really comfortable and just stop. I watched a video online one night by Sheryl Sandberg, Facebook's COO, and one thing she said that struck me was, "We run out of gas and we don't re-fuel." I didn't know who Ms. Sandberg was back then, but I lived that ideology.

I went from working in various retail stores one after the other, dealing with crazy managers and being treated unfairly on numerous occasions. One manager had me cleaning the backroom for weeks; she made me her personal store slave and treated me like shit. Regardless, I came in everyday with integrity and did what I needed to do. In the back of my mind I was creating experiences for my resume; that helped me to keep going. I refused to show any negative feelings toward the job because I had my reasons as to why I was doing it; why complain? I also felt like negative thinking was a form of weakness.

Even when it seems as if the ship is sinking, I've always had a way of showing another picture, that life is still good no matter what. I give people a chance to prove me wrong but once that time is up, you can't get it back. I wasn't happy with that first job so it didn't take me long to look for other options; on to the next! You have to believe in where you want to go and what you want out of life. I had to do what I had to do in order to get closer to my dreams. I knew it was far away, but every day, with every sacrifice I was getting closer. For every experience you'll learn a lesson and for me, I learned not to feel sorry for myself because nobody's going to feel sorry for me.

No matter how much you dislike your job, remember why you're doing it, look at the bigger picture – think positive. I don't encourage staying somewhere where you're unhappy but take the time to be at least thankful for the littlest things like having a job (because many people everyday struggle to find one) and then figure out the next plan.

Speaking of sacrifice, I want to share another story.

Once I had a job with real crappy hours and I only got to see my son for half an hour every day. I started work just before he got home from school and I would get home every night at 2 am. The only time I got to see my son was in the morning when I had to get him ready for school. Obviously, I didn't enjoy that. Women have to make hard decisions and sacrifice all the time (I think it's a part of us that we should embrace) compared to a vast majority of men (not trying to bash the guys out there just stating facts). We often have to choose our jobs over our family, our boss over our children. And when we get home, we're still making sacrifices. I had to sacrifice time with my son so that I could provide for him. I was single then – so I was playing both mother and father.

I did this for about almost a year until finally I got bored and fed up. I wanted more again, I needed more, and I'd already achieved the short term goal – another one to add to my resume. I was looking for the next opportunity. I wasn't happy anymore; I was already sacrificing time with my son and now my happiness was being compromised. One had to go, so on to the next venture, this time with better working hours to start. I had to believe in my reason and what I was worth. So I would stay up day and night sending out resumes, even to career positions that I wasn't qualified for because of my lack of education. You know what, because I believed in myself, those were the jobs that actually called me back. I achieved a goal and found work that suited my vision and this time it wasn't retail anymore. I was getting closer to that corporate job in finance I'd been dreaming of. Had I settled and gotten comfortable with the previous job, I would've missed other opportunities and miss out on my son's childhood – it would not have been worth it. My word of advice to mothers is always put your children first. No job or money in the world can compete with your child.

While working at this job, my life changed drastically. Who would've known I would find my future husband at work!?! That's right, I know all about that office romance – when you sneak lunches together, slip each other love notes, say subliminal messages to each other that only you two understand, yup, been there too! Ironically, I was already seeing someone in a long distance relationship during this time. My future hubby knew I was off the market but he didn't care. He was persistent to have me (I'm blushing now). In short, I broke up with my boyfriend from New Jersey, and Mr. Future Hubby and I ended up together. It was only months after that he quickly moved in with me at my parent's house, and from there we started planning our family.

While we were living and working together, I got pregnant (it was a planned pregnancy). News of my pregnancy spread in the office and speculations on the identity of my baby's dada was the hot new gossip (glad to say "good" gossip and not the kind I'd been used to). I knew at that point that I really needed a career. My hubby doesn't know to this day that I dropped out of high school. To be honest, I didn't feel the need to tell him; instead I wanted to show him that it didn't matter. During my maternity, I applied to a private college as a mature student. I passed the test with flying colours and completed my Accounting and Bookkeeping Certificate. Right after I graduated I was offered a big corporate position in finance on a two year contract (Law of Attraction, it was exactly what I had written down and envisioned,) I was in charge of all the franchise accounts across Canada and other major duties with this corporation. On my first day, I had to pinch myself, and asked myself what I was doing there. I was with the bigwigs, making sound decisions and taking on projects. There was no time to second guess myself now. I was on cloud nine. Living with my parents did help. I had gotten this position in October and I bought my first home January the following year at only 21 years old. God will help those who help themselves.

I know what you're probably thinking, what happened to my son's dad? Well, he never left the picture, he was always there. It was hard to let go of the love I felt for him because it was all I had ever known, but there was no turning back. I found a wonderful man who loves and respects me and who's a great father to both my kids. Fast forward we eventually got married (on a reality show); we did everything backwards, lived together, had a baby, then got a house then got married – as you can see, society's rules don't always go well with me. I do what's good for me and my family's future. I don't need society to tell me otherwise. I play by my own rules.

Here's another story I'd also like to share because I think it's important. I really had this weird perception growing up, that as adults some things would be obsolete, like bullying. Two and a half children later, that feeling of being bullied seems to just follow me, but this time it's not high school anymore, it was in a professional environment. I had started a new job for a publishing company as an account manager a year after my contract had expired. This was after the recession, so finding a job was pretty hard and stressful; my responsibilities changed drastically in less than three years. I prayed day and night for this one to come, so it was very important to me. I was back to survival mentality and now I had two kids, another on the way, a house and a hubby to worry about.

It didn't take long for me to notice that the ladies on my team weren't very nice at all. I had no idea why. They would try to make me feel out of place by purposely excluding me from conversations and lunches and even sometimes group meetings.

I took notice to that but I don't waste energy trying to make friends at work. I'm friendly and if you're not, I'm not going to go out of my way for someone to like me. I knew exactly what these ladies were up to; my spidey senses would be off the radar, because they'd constantly be chatting about me. I wasn't there to make new friends. I'd already learned how to stand up on my own.

I played their game for a while, this time the bitch's way (and yes I do have a B.I.T.C.H in me).   In fact, that's what I did – I showed my employer what I was capable of. I redirected my focus on the objective of my job, not the office bullies. Instead of giving them the satisfaction of intimidating me, they weren't going to get an iota of fear out of my body. I started voicing my opinions business-wise and contributing ideas to help the company with their growth. They loved the ideas I presented and the way I executed them. Boy, the office bullies were more agitated every day. You can't let anyone intimidate you and make you feel uncomfortable in the work environment. You're there to represent yourself in the best way possible so keeping out of the office drama is a golden rule.

I've witnessed young interns being bullied left right and center because they are working with seniors. They feel they can't say anything out of fear. As seniors and leaders, we should have an open door policy; that's the only way we can teach young leaders to become successful as well as help the company grow. My Bitch way of handling the situation was to approach them the same way they would approach me but with more love and respect – the opposite effect I call it. Kill them with kindness.

Keeping your composure at all times, though, that I found was the challenging part. There were times when I just wanted to rip them apart. The icing on the cake is being the better person. It'll always make you feel good at the end of the work day.

There's a slight twist to the office bully story. About three months into the new job I found out I was pregnant with my third son. It was an unexpected surprise that time around but regardless I was pretty excited about it. (I actually conceived roughly the day after I got hired – that's how I celebrated getting the new job.) I hid it from my employer for a month. I did feel guilty because I was still on probation. To be honest I couldn't handle the mental stress of the thought of how my employer was going to react to the news. I could only see the office bullies having the pleasure of gossiping about my pregnancy so early into my employment. This was the least of my concerns; once again, instead of showing them I cared about their drama, I blocked that thought and focused my energy on current projects. I still had to stay focused, although I have to admit, the stress of everything was affecting my blood pressure. One night I was lying in bed and thought to myself, I am a woman and women get pregnant whether it was planned or a surprise. This should not make me any less of a woman or an employee. This is a woman's purpose, to bear children should we choose to. So I sucked it all up and finally told my boss and the rest of the team the following morning. Yes I admit that I was a bit worried about how my employer was going to react, since I'd already gotten involved in so many projects that I'd initiated. After I told my boss, I was greeted by disappointment. His reaction totally turned me off; he asked me if I had already known before taking on the job. He jokingly asked if I was desperate so that I could get benefits. My jaw fell to the ground when he I heard that.

What type of person says that? I kindly gave him a little piece of my mind and I kept it moving; I continued to do as good of a job as I would pregnant or not – no excuses.

I did feel as if my employer was being prejudiced when I broke the news of my pregnancy. I didn't allow it to affect me and let the ignorance belittle me. I am a woman first before any role I take on. A woman should not feel like she needs to second guess her pregnancy or feel like she isn't worthy to sit in a meeting room full of men, pregnant. I have my every right; just like I had my right to keep my baby and I sure as heck will exercise those rights.

I can only imagine the women out there who come across situations like this. I've been there and it was not a great experience. Unfortunately, I know it still happens and now I know exactly how to handle it from the get go. This is what I was talking about earlier when I said that life has a way of shaping us up for what's to come in the future. A lot of what I endured dealing with people helped me to be less vulnerable to appalling situations like this. I'd say to let go of that YES girl mentality and stop feeling as if you have to be apologetic for something that was beyond your control or when your intentions were pure and not meant to hurt anyone. Maybe it's why there aren't enough women in power in the business world. There's a lot of qualities I do admire in men, and that's their determination to succeed and not take things so personally. Maybe a majority of us women show too much vulnerability? I myself believe so, and it's part of just being a woman. We're vulnerable creatures but learning to harness that differentiates the role we play – you can either be a pushover or a leader.

I've been fortunate to have great bosses throughout this journey who I've also learned a lot from. I gained their respect and that's why they respected me back. I've also learned a lot by their leadership styles. I wouldn't hesitate to say that I am a confident person, not because I think I'm a know-it-all; it's because I don't know it all and I'm not afraid to sometimes be the student – life is all about learning. Positive building is a domino effect. Every position I've held, I take pride in it. I don't ever take half steps, and even if it doesn't work out, I have the satisfaction of knowing at the end of the day that I've put my all in it.

We are our own boss. Don't ever under estimate your own abilities. You can't get anywhere if you're not going to go for it. If you're a waitress with big dreams of becoming a movie star, go out there and do it. Don't believe in excuses. I really feel like if you want something so badly, you go out and get it. You make all the necessary sacrifices to go after your dreams. We have all driven before where we've tried to take short cuts and we ended up getting lost or it took longer than expected. Get back on track, press the gas and drive. I learn from my past experiences the most, whether it be as tiny as a splinter or a huge life lesson. I'm learning every day from other people, co-workers, friends, ex-friends, strangers and my own kids. All it takes is a little bit of sacrifice and some determination.

Along the way I learned the value of being a passionate and grateful person and how much that helped my spiritual and mental being. If you approach everything you do with passion and gratitude it will get you somewhere. It's the fire burning inside you, what will you do with it? Doors are always closing so you can open new ones.

Here are 5 antidotes to create a formula to help clear your energy and materialize your hearts desires.

1. Gratitude
2. Passion
3. Determination
4. Forgiveness
5. Love

However you'd like to apply them, those are your key ingredients.

By the age of 25, everything I had written when I was about 17 came true. It's funny how the Law of Attraction works, it really works! The universe hears you and feels your passion to succeed. It maps out and organizes your priorities; the universe will respond.

I am now currently working on a new path, a new chapter. I'm 29 years old and I'm happy to say I've been successful in my own way. Happily married with three kids before I was 25 – everything I had written on that paper came true. I am now acting as an ambassador for The Massey Center (the place I stayed when I was pregnant with my first son,) a mentor and I have worked on various charities to pay it forward. I'm still looking to settle down in my career path as an author and motivational speaker for young women and mothers/mothers-to-be – it's a never ending journey.

I'm sharing this with you, so you can see that society doesn't define you. I was once treated as like an outcast, just some young teenage mother but because I believed in myself and kept the five key ingredients alive in my life, I was able to rise to the occasion. Without any real credentials that our society looks for, I had to believe that I could do it – and I was determined to make it.

You too can do whatever it is you feel like doing. Remember that we were born with a gift called Will. Be confident, believe in yourself, be fearless; you will gain confidence and your perception will start to change; everything you see becomes an opportunity. If you have the advantage of finishing school and going to college, take that opportunity. You don't know how lucky you are.

CHAPTER 7

Save My Soul

"And God said to the soul; I desired you before the world began".

Mechthild of Megdeburg

Some people say being a go getter is something you acquire through life and others say it's just something that you're born with. To me, I think it's in my constitution to go after what I want. It's not easy, because sometimes you tend to lose yourself along the way. This is why I think spiritual growth is so important. You have to believe in something – believe in yourself to start. I've met so many people and some are friends, who don't believe in anything at all. "Just 9-to-5 and then we die," – that's what a friend said to me. I pitied her after she said that. I felt she gave up on everything that life has to offer and that's very sad. It's sad because life can never get boring. There's always something to be thankful for, look forward to, places to see, mysteries to unfold and experiences to live.

One of the experiences that shaped me was the day I tried to take my own life away.

My life was far from perfect. My family was somewhat dysfunctional. My parents being very educated back home, made the decision to leave everything they had so we could have a brighter future. Survival was already embedded in their mentality since the first day they arrived to Canada. All my parents cared about was putting food on the table and keeping the roof over our heads.

To be honest, I don't think they were aware of what was going with their children most of the time. I practically raised myself up, and it's not my parents fault. They had to work or else we wouldn't have had food, clothes and a home. Regardless of many rough days, our family was close. During the chapter of my life when I was going through all that dilemma with friends and my son's father, I was my own worst enemy. It was more than I thought I could handle at the time.

This was during the beginning stages of my spiritual awakening. I had no idea what was happening to me. My friend was sleeping with my boyfriend, everyone was against me and I was the bad person – I felt trapped with nowhere to go. I was once again getting bullied with non-stop prank calls till three in the morning, threatening both my son and me. My poor parents would be woken up in the middle of the night by the non-stop phone calls at 3 am. My mom would rush home every day because she was worried for my safety; there was no cellphones back then, the only way she knew I was okay was to come home and check if I was there. Whenever I did go out, I'd leave a note in the kitchen telling my mom where I was going to be, that was our form of communication over a decade ago just so she could make sure that my son and I were safe. I felt everyone was turning their back on me. People I trusted were going against me. I felt alone, I had no friends. I dropped out of high school because I honestly could not take the constant harassment.

While everyone was at school getting an education, life was teaching me valuable lessons. I had to sit there and let life teach me. I felt I had no other choice; the only way to get out of this madness was to face it.

Deep down, I was afraid but I always used to show that I was a little tough cookie. Inside I was scared to bump into people I knew that I was quarrelling with because I was afraid of my own reaction; I was a fighter with a chip on my shoulder, I was on my toes and ready to brawl if it had to come down to it. The loneliness felt so dark and cold. My son's dad didn't want anything to do with me and he didn't even seem interested in wanting to be a part of our son's life. His brother and parents were active but not him so much; I get it, he was just a teenager, but then so was I. One day, that "friend" who'd betrayed me called me and I happened to pick up the phone. She was airing out my so-called dirty laundry. I was this, I was that, and she threatened to tell the entire world about my so-called secrets like who I slept with, who I dated, you know teenage drama. She had also had my son's dad on three way a few times and he like a fool would stay on the phone. Not once would he defend me. She would call me to harass me and she'd make a point that he was also on the phone (he just clung to people who disliked me because he didn't have it in his heart to forgive me for hurting him). Teenager or now as an adult – I still feel it in my heart that he could've stuck up for me because I was more than his friend, I was his son's mother, who was at the time struggling to be the best mother to his own while battling my own inner demons; anyone threatening me and his son should've been out of the question. I swear at that time, he would've rather I was dead.

I remember that day like it was yesterday, I've never felt so alone in my life. "What's happening to me? " I asked myself. "I am such a good mother to my son, I know that I'm a good person – why are they making me feel like this?" I started to question this so-called God that I believed in all my life. I felt He must know how I am feeling, and He must know I am ready to give up. Where was He, I needed to be saved? Why was this happening to a good person? I had enough. I was ready; I was ready to give up the fight. I've always had to act tough because I had no choice, but this time, I didn't want to be tough anymore. I didn't want to put up a fight. I didn't want to face the battle. I kept a lot of stuff away from my mom because I didn't want her to worry. This time, the battle was over, I didn't have anymore strength in me to fight it. I was giving up and I was allowing myself to crumble. All walls down, bare and naked I was vulnerable.

The worst of the worst thoughts came into my head; I didn't want to live. It was all too painful. My friends all turned their backs on me, nobody was there for me anymore, and my son's dad made it clear to me that He didn't have my back or give a shit about my well-being – that was the last straw for me.

After that phone call, everything just hit me. I hung up the phone, dropped to the floor and started crying hysterically. I lost my mind. I ran to my kitchen and at this point, I was already gone as if my soul left me, everything was a blur. I remember opening the drawer where my dad kept all his meat knives and pulled out the shiniest one. I walked down the hall to our powder room where my dad kept all the medication and grabbed everything I could. Drugs and sharp knife in my hand,

I ran back upstairs to my room, tears rolling down my cheeks. I opened up all the medication I had grabbed from the cabinet, emptied it out into my hand and swallowed them all. Opened up another and swallowed whatever was left. I didn't want to feel the pain, so I thought maybe if I overdosed and cut myself, it wouldn't be that painful. So I took an entire bottle of Tylenol to end it and swallowed them all.

I was ready; I was ready to cut myself. At this point, I was already groggy. I remember my head bobbling back and forth as I reached out for the knife. Cut, I tried to cut my wrist. Cut again, the first time wasn't deep enough. I cut a little deeper and this time the intention and strength to just bleed to death. Then I don't know what happened but I am assuming the drugs knocked me out. All I remember was waking up on the floor with the knife next to me, foamy mouth and meds everywhere. This was all happening while my son was at daycare and my parents were at work and my siblings were at school. I looked over and there was a phone. I reached out for it, and I called a buddy of mine in Miami. It must have been meant to be, he answered. He was happy to hear my voice but he could tell there was something really wrong. I told him, I just tried to kill myself and I don't know what happened and my wrist was bleeding. He was hysterical but I couldn't grasp anything he was saying. All I understood was, you need to get out, come here, I will wire you some money and you take a flight from Buffalo. That sounded so good to me at that time because I felt like he was the only one who really truly cared for me. All I wanted was that feeling that someone cared about how I was feeling, someone who understands. I don't know how, but I managed to get up. My wrist was cut but only bled as if I got pricked by rose thorns. I then packed my bag, a picture of my son and an album that I created when he was first born. I remember just standing there over my bed; just looking at this one photo of my son, then took his baby blanket, sniffed his scent and shoved it in my bag. I was going to leave this baby behind that I loved oh so much, and all these thoughts started going through my head. I will never see this beautiful baby ever again or my family but I felt okay at the same time. It was a selfish act, I felt I deserved better but in reality I didn't deserve them. I wasn't in harmony, I was lacking inner peace – I didn't know who I was anymore.

I packed my stuff and left. I was groggy the entire time; I vomited in my mouth a couple times on my ride to the bus station. There was a place where I could retrieve my wired money, so I cashed out and bought my one way ticket; I was a hot mess. Here I am 16 years old, red puffy eyes, no makeup (I looked like I was probably 12) and one little bag. I had gotten on the bus and people were looking at me funny. Here's this little 5 foot girl, 90 lbs., who looks about 12. I was too upset to think rationally. I wanted to escape; the thought of killing myself was starting to turn me off but the thought of running away felt more empowering. While on the bus, I was starting to feel really sick and I kept going to the washroom to vomit. I was getting even groggier than I had felt earlier to the point I started hyperventilating and got extremely light headed. I kept fighting it off with thoughts of starting a new life and meeting new friends. I thought of what I could do with my new friends to prevent this from happening again but it all came down to building the walls, not trusting anyone to come into my life at all – I had it all figured out I thought. To this day I can't imagine how my parents felt. My dad doesn't say much, but I know deep down he too was in disarray. I left a bloody scene in my bedroom, with empty medication bottles and a knife; and me nowhere to be found. By the time my parents came home, I was already on my way to cross the US border. I wasn't sure at the time why my mother never called the cops. Maybe she had an intuition not to.

The speakers had come on the bus and woke me up. I'm not sure if I had been knocked out from all the drugs or if I'd just fallen asleep – probably a combination of both. "Please get your passports ready, we are now approaching immigration!"

"This is it, freedom," I thought "I can now start a new life." Then a sense of sadness came over me, when a vision of my little boy popped up in my head. I right away ignored it; there was no turning back now, I must leave, and there was nothing for me left. I dropped out of school, my name was tarnished, now everybody just wants to fight me or be against me and I felt nobody cared for me or respected me. The lights came on the bus. I picked up my bag, took a deep breath and lined up with the rest.

"Hello," said the immigration officer. I looked up trying not to look him in the eye and said hello right back, trying to force a smile.

He checked my passport and all my paperwork. He paused for awhile. He asked me where I was going. I lied and said I was going to see family. He again paused and asked to see my bag. He first pulled out the framed picture of my son, and then he pulled out his blanket and the baby album. He asked me who these were. I answered softly and said my son; I felt the pain at that point right in my chest, as if an archer just shot me with his bow and arrow. He told me to hang on, and he went to talk to some other officers. I knew at that point I was in shit. First of all, I was under age but I thought deep down because I had a son that I was an adult now, that's how it had been – I didn't need a guardian to sign my papers anymore even though I was under the age of 18. While the immigration guy was talking to his peers, crazy thoughts were running through my mind a mile a second. I thought I was going to be detained; I was going to be checked in at some kind of crazy ward. All I knew is that I didn't want to go back. Twenty minutes later, he came back, he says to me, "Sorry but you're under age and we can't let you in the country. You're going to have to wait here and we will get you on the next bus back to Toronto." I honestly didn't know how I felt at that point – a failure, I was being forced to go back and face myself. Deep down, I felt safe but at the same time, I didn't want to face anyone. I became a coward. I was afraid of everything.

It was about 3:30 am. There was something that helped me that night, I don't know what. I don't even remember how I got home, and I had no money. For some odd reason, I made it back to my parent's front door. I rang the door bell, and I can hear heavy footsteps. It was my mom. She opened the door and said, "Thank you God." Her prayers were answered that night. She and my aunt stayed up all night praying for me to come back. I was exhausted and nobody asked me questions. Instead my aunt and my mother sat at the foot of my bed and said, "Don't let these people bring you down. God will never put anything in your life that you cannot handle. You're a strong young woman with a beautiful child. These so-called friends aren't worth it; you're blessed."

The following evening, I was in my room just lying down, thinking about everything and trying to figure shit out. My son's dad surprisingly called me just past midnight. He was practically trying to lecture me but I wasn't even hearing it. I was incoherent. I didn't care. I felt like my soul left me. I felt cold, no love, no hate, nothing.

However, that night was the night that forever changed my life.

I was lying down talking to him, with my back turned against the window. The blinds were slightly opened but I had a few blinds on the side that were missing, so you could see right outside where the tree was. While we were talking, I felt the hairs on my back stand up. I felt this heavy, I mean heavy presence; it wasn't the kind of presence you feel when you feel like someone's watching you, it was unexplainable. It was much more empowering than frightening; I didn't feel scared at all. All of a sudden I heard a soft voice almost as if was telepathically speaking to me. I heard, "Turn around, turn around, turn to me." I ignored it at first because I was trying to listen to my son's dad lecture me, but then I heard it again. "Turn to me."

I turned around and for some odd reason I looked straight out the window where the tree was. I could not believe what I saw. The moment I saw it, tears started dropping from my eyes uncontrollably. I remember my heart racing. I dropped the phone and I was saying in complete shock, "Oh my God, Oh my God." In the background I can still hear my son's dad on the phone line sounding worried. "Hello, hello, what's happening, are you there?" he asked.

I turned around again and this time I rubbed my eyes and

counted to three "1, 2, 3!" It was still there, radiating from the tree like the sun. It was about 2 am at this point and it was pitch dark. I dropped down to my knees and I cried, I cried like I never cried before but it felt so good. There he was, Jesus! Yes, I said Jesus. I saw Jesus. The tree bush was illuminated like the sun, and there I could see his face, the same face you see on the crucifix. His head was looking down and he looked sad. He wasn't made out of flesh or anything; he looked golden as if he was really made from the sun.

I rubbed my eyes over and over again while crying hysterically. I only had that one split-second where I asked myself if this was really, really real. Then no thoughts entered my mind... I was one with Jesus. No words, no questions asked, still on my knees, I stared and cried. Like I said, I don't know how long this apparition lasted but it was real. I remember lying back down as if nothing had happened and picked up the phone (my son's dad was still there). He was concerned, "What happened, what happened?" he asked. I felt at peace, like everything I had gone through ever in my life that ever hurt me was gone and I somehow had this universal understanding of it all. I answered him with, "Nothing" and that was it.

You know that saying, only give yourself to Jesus or only Jesus can save your soul; that night I understood that. I tried to take my life away and he saved me. He saved my soul.

Years later my eldest son's father still remembers that night and it wasn't until maybe almost a decade later that I actually told him. He doesn't understand what happened either. It's a bit farfetched to grasp anyway, so I didn't expect him or anyone to understand it, yet alone believe it. I know it was real and I've always felt a bond with Jesus. Even as a child I'd experienced other apparitions very similar to this with words and messages. I still get them and I tell my most trusted person – my mother.

It really makes me think of our existence here. It's so much deeper than a 9-to-5 or what we see in the media. There's so much more and to think, I was going to take my own life away.

Whenever you feel like giving up, just remember that there is always a light that shines at the end of it all. This light knows, this light sees and this light will help you overcome anything – and it is the Love of God the creator. It's not a religious thing I'm trying to put out here; I'm trying to unite everyone through love. To reach that, we have to value our own life first and understand it.

One thing's for certain, there is a God; I believe in Jesus and that we have a purpose here on earth. There's a reason why he kept me alive. Whatever that reason is, I just trust in my heart that it will come about. At the end of the day, I'm only a vessel, a soul in my body and I have a Will to carry out. With that being said, I feel it is important to always uplift people you meet because you never know what they're battling with. Walk with the light, be the light and you will see the light.

CHAPTER 8

The Real Honey Lou

"To be yourself in a world that is constantly trying to make you something else is the greatest accomplishment."
Ralph Waldo Emerson

Oh yes, I remember the day when my momma said we were going to Canada.

I was about four years old when my parents decided that was the best thing they could do for us. Canada, I had never heard of, only when my mother was on the phone talking to some strange person that later figured out was my aunt who sponsored us (we are in gratitude for our Auntie Fe). Heck, what did I know? All I knew was, I was heading on a boat and going away for a long time. I grew up with my Nanan and my other aunt Rita, the two women who I adore so much and who will always hold a special place in my heart. My aunt was like a mother to me as she didn't have any kids of her own.

The day has come; we arrive at the pier. There was a huge gigantic boat docked about 100 meters from us. It was blue with some rust crawling up from the waters below it. I have never been on a boat, I thought. Then all of a sudden, a feeling of loneliness hit me. I was six years old then – since a young age I've always been very in tune with my feelings. I had this intuition that I was never going to see my Nanan and my aunt ever again. I remember feeling alone and crying; I refused to let my Nanan's soft gentle wrinkled hands go.

In my early years, I was actually closer to my auntie Rita and my Nanan than to my own mother; my mother doesn't see it that way but that's how I felt and still feel today. I knew my auntie Rita as my mother for the first six years of my life. Although my own mother was present, I felt more connected to my aunt Rita. I spent a lot of time with her and my Nanan, more than I did with my mother. My aunt Rita owned a store and a few businesses back home that she inherited from great-great aunts and it was just recently handed down to my mother when Aunt Rita passed in 2011. She never had any children and had never gotten married, so I was like her only child. Her life was so committed to running the businesses that she sacrificed her own love and happiness; it was a promise to our great aunts and it's said to be cursed with their blood over 100 years ago (to this day it's still standing strong).

I remember her holding me tightly and gently squeezing my hands as if she knew she wasn't going to see me for a long time, or maybe even forever as we stood there gazing at the gigantic ship. I could hear her almost begging my mom to let me stay as they murmured words to each other back and forth. I looked back to only see my Nanan from a distance, trying to hold in her tears as we slowly started to walk towards the boat. Something came over me. I let go of my Aunt Rita's hands and I ran to my Nanan, clinging on to her legs as the wind blew her sundress on my face. I said I didn't want to leave. At that point, my other siblings intervened and bribed me with empty promises. It was ten years before I saw my auntie Rita and Nanan again and unfortunately that was the last time.

We were now boarding a plane to Toronto and I had already forgotten about my motherland due to the excitement of going on a plane and finally seeing Canada, the land of promises. It was still spring in early June of 1990, I remember breathing in the air and it even smelled and tasted different. I closed my eyes and took a long deep breath and took in the fresh air, exhaling with a small grin on my face. Now my friends this was the start of a new journey, my life and my trials and tribulations. I already felt it through my toes, right to the crown of my head. Who am I, and who was I going to become? My journey was just getting started and this is exactly where I was supposed to be.

I pretty much grew up as a normal kid. My parents are blue collar people who worked their butts off to support their four children. I didn't have much growing up, no fancy clothes or shoes; I probably only remember going back to school shopping twice ever in my life. I can almost still feel that innocence in me, when I used to make dollhouses made of shoeboxes and that was enough to make me happy; going back to the nostalgic feeling of being a kid without having the responsibilities we have as an adult.

I don't think I was a spoiled kid or an entitled little brat but I was born with a spoiled attitude and I think it's because I always knew what I wanted and freely expressed it. My family is a bit dysfunctional at times and I've come to believe that this is normal; there's no such thing as a perfect family however there is a happy family. Both parents held degrees back home but had to find just any job in Canada so they could survive. What they did for us was pretty selfless. I couldn't imagine myself right now, moving my family to a foreign country, and starting my whole life again – that takes a lot of courage. I admire them so much for that and that is mainly the reason I idolized them from day one.

For the last 20 years and counting, my parents have had the same routine; get up at 5 o'clock in the morning and get home by 6 o'clock in the evening from work. We lived with my aunt but not for long, within six months they had kicked us out and told my parents they needed to find a place to live. We lived in a small apartment with two bedrooms; my parents had one and all four of us had to share the other. Two years later my parents bought a little town home and by that time I'd already moved to my third school. I have many fond memories there; it's where I grew up.

Since my parents were gone for the majority of the time, I had a lot of freedom to do whatever I wanted. With freedom, you can do anything and that's where I got to experiment with things per se and test life. I pretty much raised myself. I'm admitting that I lacked guidance growing up; I guided myself by playing with fire and getting burned. After school is where I used to get into trouble. I joined a gang, met some bad friends and I became ruthless.

Growing up wasn't always easy when I didn't understand half of the things that were going on at home. There was couple of times where I saw my brother try to kill himself. The first time was just before we moved into our new home. We were all in the living room watching TV and I couldn't help but notice some loud banging in the washroom. I then tried to open it but it was locked. I asked my parents to come by the washroom to listen to the weird bangs coming from the inside. They called out his name but nothing. I was the only one who knew how to pick the lock (yes I was that kid that picked all the locks on the door), so I picked it and opened it and there I saw my brother, lying at the foot of the tub, bleeding from knife wounds, his eyes rolled back and his mouth foaming. There was blood coming out his nose and mouth. I started screaming and I called everyone for help. That was the first negative incident I was ever exposed to. My stomach churned and that memory used to play in my head for a long time. There are certain things you don't really understand in life until you actually go through it Thank God the ambulance was well-timed and they were able to keep him alive. I questioned it in the back of my mind, as to why would anyone want to kill themselves. Could life really get that hard and ugly?

Where I grew up, the kids in school were a bit on the tougher side. It was the kind of school where people will take advantage of you at your most vulnerable time. So, I learned to be tough myself. Here I was, small, bony, and I was always the shortest in my class. I looked fragile and maybe that's why the kids at school thought they could robotically pick on me. Their actions already didn't resonate with me; I just knew that I didn't want to be that person getting bullied.

One story I'd like to share was the time I was ganged up on at school. With so much online bullying that's happening in this day and age, I think it's important to touch on this subject and what I had to go through as well. This was actually just one of many incidents that really stuck out for me.

I was in the eighth grade to be exact and I went from being everyone's friend to being the girl the entire school picked on. It all happened overnight. I'd been at my elementary school for about five years and accomplished so much there. I was a smart kid, captain of most of the sports teams, and I was looking forward to getting an award at my graduation of some sort. That was my goal so I could make my mother proud.

That didn't happen at all, it was quite the opposite actually. Months leading up to my graduation I moved to another school because I was being bullied. Every day I would come to school and nobody would talk to me. There was one girl who was the mastermind of it all – go figure she used to be my best friend; you know what they say, keep your friends close and your enemies closer. I went from being the most liked popular person in the entire school to everyone turning their backs on me – for no real reason. I was the hottest topic of gossip, they called me nasty names to my face and they'd make a point to embarrass me.

Inside I had to try to keep it all in and act like it didn't daunt me. I wanted to be that tough girl that everyone thought I was – that was the hardest thing to do. During sport try outs, they would literally throw the ball away and stop the game to rant and put me on the spot. Every time they passed it to me, they would whip it at me. Of course I'd fight back and ask them what their problem was but at the same time... I didn't want to add more fuel to the fire. Every day for about five months I had to deal with it. Again, when I'd get home and lie in my bed at night the darkness crossed my mind, wanting to end my life as the image of my own brother trying to take his own would replay in my head over and over again; evil was trying to get me. I was so alone at school, that the fat girl I used to bully was my only friend – funny how the tables turn.

I was also disappointed in the teachers as well, I honestly thought they'd intervene and try to add some water to the fire. The teachers were clearly aware of what was going on but did nothing to help rectify the situation. I felt like they hated me too – I could taste the loneliness as if I licked the blood off my wounds. It came to the point where I just had enough, either I was going to get into a physical fight or just remove myself from the situation. The bullying was getting so intense that I started skipping school.

A decision had to be made at this point. I just wanted to be happy and not wake up every day stepping on eggshells and always having to watch my back. The false rumors, the writing in the change rooms, the nonstop prank calls and threats – I'd had enough of it all. I was ready to explode and let the darkness take over me.

I thought to myself while walking home one day, why I should even stick around? I wanted to choose happiness over this cloud of misery. I finally confided in my mother and told her how I felt. My mother is very supportive in nature and she could feel my hurt, pain and desperation. She suggested that I transfer to another school; she was worried about my safety. I agreed and thought that was the only option I had. I was ready to let go of my ego and move somewhere else where I could get control back in my life. I just wanted to be normal again.

At that young age, I'd already figured out a lot of things. The #1 lesson was to treat everyone fairly. Until it happens to you, you don't know what the other person is feeling. #2. Don't trust just anybody with your secrets and #3. Move quickly and change your environment before it becomes a bigger problem. To this day I still keep those life lessons close and I'm always making similar decisions in my life; nowadays I don't hesitate to make the changes. I never really had a problem making new friends; it was maintaining the friendships and trusting them. I was going into this new school with new wisdom that I'd learned from my mistakes and from others. I felt even more empowered. I consciously applied the lessons I learned, hoping not to make the same mistake twice.

Bullying comes in so many various forms. At the new school, I was faced with another challenge and this time it wasn't my classmates. It was the teachers. The teachers looked at me as if I was this little troublemaker, literally treating like an outcast (I was no troublemaker, I just learned to be a little bit more outspoken). The principal at the new school (she was evil) had it out for me from the day I set foot in her school. She was prejudiced towards me and hated me without even knowing a single thing about me. And, she was not afraid to let everyone know that.

I was already sort of depressed but I hid it from everyone and it didn't help. During a class trip, the principal for some odd reason took me by my jacket, picked me up and threw me in front of the bus. I had no clue why I was in trouble but that's what she did. She and a handful of teachers would talk about me in the halls – I'd catch them. The French teacher and the principal once called my parents in to the school for a drawing that I had done for my birthday invitation that they thought was too explicit – mind you the inspiration came from the girl group TLC. They had given me detention for it, for God knows how long and called my parents into the office. They had told my parents that I needed help.

Help for what? Maybe they could've paid attention to how well drawn my art was and encouraged me to draw more instead of telling them I needed help! It was a battle with the principal and the teachers for four months leading up to my graduation and if it hadn't been such a short period of time, I would have probably moved again. But what would that do for me if I always ran away from my problems? That was the start of this perception that I was a wild child. Some of my friends' parents thought I was a bad influence and disliked me; I used to ask myself why, when I am the most loyal, caring and loving person in the world. There was something dark that was projecting out of me and I didn't know what it was. I didn't understand it at all, because in comparison, their children were doing a lot worse than I was, they were just good at hiding it. Because of all the bullying, prejudice and stereotyping, a "bad" child was born; there is some truth that stemmed from it. After trying to prove myself to others, I was tired of it. I decided I wasn't going to give an EFF anymore. I was just going to be me and stop trying to pretend just to please others; if they didn't like me, then too bad so sad because I was going to love me.

I didn't care whether they liked me or not. I'm not perfect but I can tell you I'd be the first to give you the shirt off my back. I have nothing to prove to anyone. I knew in the back of my mind the kind of person I wanted to become and I knew the essence of my soul. There was no need to get up in people's faces to get approval. I was going to live 'me' whether they liked it or not.

And that's what I've done.